To Tom,

all the best,
from all at wing...

Kind regards.

Bob Shawroch.

Vincent Bau...
Harold Hayfield.

Best wishes
Edith & Muriel

Len Benenshaw.

Hope you will be
back with us
soon & good morning,
proper, best you when you
best. wishes
Yours

Martin Berkenshaw

Float Fishing with
Ivan Marks

Float Fishing with Ivan Marks

Ivan Marks &
John Goodwin

Pelham Books
London

First published in Great Britain by
Pelham Books Ltd
52 Bedford Square, London W.C.1
January 1978
Second impression April 1979

ISBN 0 7207 1027 8

Filmset in 11pt Baskerville by
D.P. Media Limited, Hitchin.
Printed and bound in Great Britain by
Billing & Sons Limited, Guildford, London and Worcester.

To Christopher

Contents

List of Illustrations   8

Acknowledgments   10

1   Float Fishing with Ivan   11
    by John Goodwin

2   The Basics   26

3   My Floats and How I Fish Them   50
    Part 1 – Floats for Running Waters
    Part 2 – Floats for Still and Slow-moving Waters

4   The Secrets of My Success   148

    Postscript   169
    by John Goodwin

    Index   173

Illustrations

		page
1	Stick float	55
2	Basic shotting pattern for a stick float fished at a depth of less than 6 feet	57
3	Basic shotting pattern for a stick float fished at a depth of over 6 feet	58
4	Carrot	61
5	Basic shotting for a Carrot fished at a depth of less than 6 feet	62
6	Pacemaker	65
7	Basic shotting for a Pacemaker	66
8	Avon	68
9	An Avon float shotted to fish a fairly deep and turbulent water	70
10	Balsa	72
11	A Balsa float shotted to fish a fast turbulent water	73
12(a)	Swinger – Set 1	76
12(b)	Swinger – Set 2	77
13	Typical shotting for a Swinger float	79
14	Arrow	81
15	Typical shotting for an Arrow float	83
16	Ducker	85
17	Ducker float shotted for reverse trotting	87
18	Waggler	89

19	Under-tow	93
20	Special Balsa	97
21	Typical shotting for a Special Balsa float	99
22	Marksman	104
23	Dart	106
24	2 mm (short, canal) antenna	109
25	Typical shotting for a 2 mm antenna	111
26	2 mm (long, canal) antenna	113
27	2 mm Slimline antenna	115
28	Javelin	117
29	Typical shotting for a Javelin float	118
30	Tipped Swinger	120
31	Typical shotting for a reed antenna float	124
32(a)	Reed antenna – Set 1	127
32(b)	Reed antenna – Set 2	128
33	Tipped antenna	130
34	Reverse Ducker	132
35	Missile	134
36	Typical shotting for a Missile	135
37	Ordinary Zoomer	138
38	Tipped Zoomer	140
39	Typical shotting for ordinary Zoomer float	141
40	Ivan's special Zoomer	143
41	The correct shotting for Ivan's special Zoomer	145

Acknowledgments

The authors would like to express their gratitude to John Metcalfe for supplying the illustrations for the book.

1 Float Fishing with Ivan
by John Goodwin

I think that deep down my preference for float fishing is connected with my personality.

Ivan Marks on Match Fishing

WHEN IVAN AND I were preparing his book on match fishing we had to try to cover the whole field as comprehensively as possible. At the time it was one of my regrets that we were unable to give more space to what is undoubtedly one of Ivan's greatest talents – the ability to catch fish on a float. It became obvious to me that it is in this fundamental skill that he excels more than in any other, and it is therefore with a good deal of pleasure that I have this opportunity to help him with a full-length book on the subject.

Of course, I knew he was good. Don't we all? I don't think anyone would disagree with the statement that there is not a better float angler alive today. Even his critics would admit that. But until recently I didn't realise just how unarguably he is in a class all on his own. At various times over the last twenty years I have fished alongside, or watched, most of the top names in fishing. But Ivan is something altogether different. When he is in full flow, not messing about as he sometimes does, but really turning it on, watching him is like

watching a great artist at work. The casting, the float control, the smooth striking, landing and unhooking of fish, the
feeding and tackle adjustments are all blended into an effort-
less performance which looks supremely relaxed and simple.
When he is in the mood Ivan can turn the everyday craft of
float fishing into something beautiful – rhythmic, certain,
perfect. It must be a very rare gift.

Any angler who has come across Ivan in this mood in a
competition will know exactly what I mean. I know of one
very good and experienced matchman who sat beside Ivan
one day when the fish, and Ivan, were really on song. Ivan
annihilated him, and the man was in such a demoralised
state afterwards that he actually gave up match fishing. 'I
realised', he said, 'for the first time what class is all about.
You can't compete with magic – and that's what he is, he's a
bloody magician!'

A couple of years ago I was fishing a stillwater not far from
my home. It was one of those dreary days when the fish were
so unresponsive that the dozen or so anglers present became
restless. A man near me spoke in a loud, complaining voice
to anyone who cared to listen: 'I've been here since six,' he
said bitterly, 'and I've tried everything. The lot. I don't
reckon you could catch 'em with five pound notes today.'

Another man, more reasonable, said amiably, 'Maybe
we're not doing it right. I bet somebody could catch them.'

The first man was indignant. 'I'll tell you what,' he said,
'what I should like just now is to see one of those know-alls
here and see how they get on. One of these experts.' He said
the word with the maximum of sarcasm. 'Like Ivan Marks.
Now you don't see him in places like this where the fish are
hard to catch. I'll bet you anything you like he'd be as
stumped as we are!'

I remember this typical little scene so well because only a
few weeks ago I took Ivan to that very place. The pity was

that the Moaner was not there. But apart from his absence things were very much the same – about a dozen anglers sitting disconsolately on their baskets with hardly a sprat to show between them.

They had had the best part of the day: it was after ten when we arrived and the sun was beginning to get hot. The purpose of our visit was for Ivan to demonstrate his tipped antenna floats and he was not particularly setting out to catch a lot of fish. We had chosen this place as being fairly quiet and with the opportunity of fishing far out if necessary. It was also necessary to find a place where Ivan would not be crowded with admirers.

For some minutes Ivan cast around to find the exact position of a shelf. When he found it; about thirty yards out, he settled down to feed the area quietly with casters in groundbait. Each time he cast, the tipped antenna sailed delicately across the water to land always in an area no bigger than a dustbin lid. He didn't seem to aim it, it just went there. The float cocked gently in three barely discernible stages until the merest dot of the tipped insert rode fleetingly among the ripples. After ten minutes I began to get a headache.

Ivan meantime was happily feeding his swim, occasionally making tackle adjustments and smoking a cigarette with the contented air of a man who just knew that he was going to catch some fish. He was right. Gradually they came, not big fish at first, but increasing in size each time. By the end of an hour he was beginning to make it look easy. During the second hour the landing net was called for on several occasions and a buzz of discussion could be heard around the bank. Suddenly Ivan struck into a really good fish which fought strongly. As he was playing it, two or three men, unable to resist the temptation any longer, came slinking round to watch it being landed. They said nothing as he

eventually unhooked it and put it in his keepnet. He re-cast
and sat watching his float in that famous casual manner of
his. Another man put down his rod and walked over. He was
joined by the owner of the water, a man I know to be
particularly hard to impress, but who now stood watching
with his eyes on stalks as Ivan landed yet another good fish.
Again Ivan resumed fishing unconcernedly and the silence
was becoming unbearable. But I knew when the conversa-
tion did begin it would be delightful. It was.

'Where's your float then, mate?'

'Out there, look.' Ivan pointed.

There was a great squinting across the ripples. No one
could see it. Obligingly Ivan pulled it in and cast it out again.
As it cocked and almost submerged there was more squinting and muttering.

'You must have X-ray eyes!'

Casually Ivan struck into antoher good fish from a bite
that nobody had seen. He landed it and prepared to re-bait.

'What bait are you using then?'

'Casters.' Ivan held out a handful. 'Have you got any?
You can have some of these if you like.' He pointed to a
gallon container full of first-class casters.

'Hmmm! What size hook have you got on?'

'A 22. Look.' Ivan displayed the minute hook on the palm
of his hand. The man seemed to have difficulty in seeing it
even from a matter of inches. Words failed him.

One of the men beckoned me aside and addressed me in a
whisper. 'This is upsetting me', he said, looking worried.
'I've only started fishing this year, and I thought I was doing
quite well. Till now.' He looked across at Ivan as if he were
gazing at something from another planet.

I tried to reassure him. 'Look,' I said, 'not to worry. You
wouldn't expect to be as good as him. None of us are. He's
what you might call a professional. But if you go and ask him

how he's doing it he'll tell you.' The man looked doubtful.
'Go on', I said. 'He won't mind.'

Very patiently and helpfully Ivan explained everything
the man wanted to know. He showed him all the terminal
tackle, discussed his choice of float, showed him how to cast
and pointed out that it was an easy water to fish anyway.
Which it wasn't. I heard another of the onlookers trudging
back to his swim, and his empty net, complaining to another
that hooks like that were ridiculous and how he always used
a size 16. He added that if the fish were going to bite they'd
pull under one float as good as another. Whereupon he
pulled his own lighthouse from the water and thrashed it out
again. As Ivan began to pack up I reflected that there was no
hope for that man, but there was hope for the one who had
asked Ivan all the questions. He came up to me again and
said quietly: 'Who is he, then?'

'It's Ivan Marks', I said. 'Have you heard of him?' I
thought the man was going to fall down on his knees. His
eyes shone.

'Well, stone me!' he said. 'Just wait till I tell them at work.
They'll never believe me.' He thought for a moment then
added, 'I'm glad it was him. I don't mind so much now.' He
went off a happy man, and all in all it was well nigh a perfect
day except that the Moaner had not been there.

Catching those fish that day had impressed the other
anglers enormously, but it had been nothing to Ivan. He
hadn't been trying particularly. To him it was easy fishing,
no pressure from anglers around him, just a hard-fished but
not a well-fished water. He hadn't even bothered to change
floats. It frightens me to think what he could have done if he
had really been in earnest. Like the day we fished the match
stretch of the Witham.

The fish there are nobody's mugs, as many of you will
know. But as it happened the circumstances combined to

produce from Ivan a quite stupendous performance. Maybe
it was the fact that he was fishing a big match water, maybe it
was because the fish were there and he was in the mood,
maybe it was that he saw it as a challenge – who knows?
Whatever the reasons, I was privileged to witness the finest
exhibition of float fishing that I ever expect to see, and I only
wish that all the other anglers in the country had been there
to see it as well. Seeing, they say, is believing, and quite
honestly if I had not seen it I would never have believed it. I
live close to the Witham, I must have spent thousands of
hours fishing it and I thought I had seen it all. But I was
wrong.

It was late in July, mid-week. The hemp and tares season
was at its peak on the Witham, and as anyone will tell you,
casters are a second bait there until September. So I took
some tares. We were out to catch roach.

Ivan heaved his assortment of tackle from the car, and the
springs rose with relief. He staggered down to the water's
edge with his enormous basket and when he opened the lid it
was like something out of a cartoon inside. He ferreted
around among boxes, spools of line, reels, bits of floats, tins
and everything but the kitchen sink. He grinned. 'It's all
here somewhere', he said happily, and proceeded to sur-
round himself with stuff that looked as if it might have been a
fifty pence job lot at an auction.

I'd seen this before. I wasn't deceived. He looked across
the Witham at a few roach rising in the ripples. He rubbed
his hands. 'I shall catch', he said, simply. Looking back I
would say that must have been the understatement of the
year. He uncovered his gleaming bucket of casters and asked
me what I was going to use as bait.

'Tares', I said.

'I'm surprised at you,' he said, 'using those nasty little
seeds. I'm going to use casters.'

I was just a little bit shaken. I was quite sure, at that time of the year, and in that particular place, that he was making a mistake.

For the first half hour it looked as though I was right. The roach there had been educated to tares. I was into them virtually from the first cast and Ivan was definitely struggling. It was as well that I enjoyed the first half hour because from then on I began to feel slightly sick. During the second half hour Ivan caught me up, and after that it was just murder. I was still catching steadily but Ivan was slaughtering them. I reckon on that day I caught roach fast enough to win a lot of matches, and certainly I was fishing to my limit. Under any other circumstances I would have been very pleased with myself, and yet Ivan was just playing with me. In the end, despite having put on one of my best performances, I felt just like the man at the stillwater. I packed up and went over to Ivan. 'Right,' I said, 'just show me how!' So, he moved up a few pegs and started from scratch again. When he'd finished, two hours later, I had seen every single thing that he had done, and he had told me why. And yet I knew that I could never do it myself if I lived to be a thousand. That is a very hard thing for an experienced angler to have to admit, but it has to be faced. A good angler is a million miles away from a great angler. The Ivan Marks of this world are born, not made. Let me tell you what happened.

He began fishing the middle, maybe a bit beyond, with a tipped antenna and a size 22 hook. Initially he shotted the last four feet of his tackle with quite a lot of small shot in groups and he was quite precise in making sure that the last shot was fishing just clear of the bottom. He fed casters in groundbait very regularly in small quantities, working up to a time when he was loose-feeding casters by a ratio of three to one.

So far I was able to keep in touch. But then he began changing the position of his working shot until he got a bite. If he did not then get another bite next cast, he was altering depth and shot again, and he refused to be satisfied until he could get a bite a cast. He would then continue fishing until he failed to get another bite. Immediately there would be a change of shotting and this went on throughout the whole session.

At the same time he was drawing the fish closer. After an hour he had brought them to within three or four rod lengths out, had changed floats twice and was still insisting on a bite a cast. At the end of an hour and half he had that shoal right at his rod end, queuing up. Once he had them going like this he was merciless. All the constant actions, the feeding, casting, striking, unhooking of fish, re-baiting, altering depth, moving shot, were done with the minimum of fuss. It all looked so incredibly easy. Every time he altered his tackle his catching rate increased. As far as I could tell he never made a mistake: it was as if he had the fish on a piece of elastic, almost as if he could see right under the water, even into their minds. He might have been one of them.

When he had them at his rod tip, fishing like a machine, it would have been enough. You might say it was a classic demonstration of how it should be done. But for Ivan it was not enough. He can never be satisfied. Ignoring the fact that he had a roach pole with him, he then took the bottom section off his four-piece rod, reel and all, tied the line to the bottom ring of the second section and proceeded to bring the fish in still further. He was then catching nine feet from the bank.

After a few minutes of this he took the second section off his rod and tied his line direct to the last ring of the third section. He changed floats and caught fish six feet from the bank. All the time the meticulous feeding pattern had been

kept up and the depth and shotting altered without losing
the rate of a bite a cast. Surely, I thought, this it it. But no!
Minutes later he took apart the last two sections of his rod,
tied the line to the bottom ring of the tip section, lit a
cigarette, used the spent match as a float, and with this
incredible combination proceeded to take quality roach from
the match length of the Witham fishing literally inches from
his wellingtons. By this time I can tell you I would not have
been surprised to see a roach crawl out of the water and take
a caster from his hand!

For half an hour he kept this up, chatting away and
completely unmoved at what he had done. Then, suddenly,
it was over. He became bored. There was nothing more to
do. He'd been asked to show what he could do, and he'd
done it. Short of catching the fish on the mud at the water's
edge he could do no more. 'Let's pack up and move somewhere else', he said. 'We shan't learn anything more here.'
As we packed up I wondered what else there might be to
learn.

I thought a lot about this afterwards. I'm a reasonably
good angler, better than some and worse than others, and in
my time I've beaten anglers next to me quite easily, and
often been beaten by them. But this performance was something different again. This was devastation bordering on the
miraculous. Small wonder that those anglers who have seen
Ivan at the top of his form will swear to you that he is
absolutely out of this world – technically perfect but highly
original with it, to be compared with nobody but himself, a
kind of genius. He has this amazing knack, when he knows
there are fish to be caught, of knowing exactly what they
want and how they want it. When the mood is on him he can
just about make a float talk and at these times he is not really
fishing against anyone else at all, he is fishing against himself, against his own standards of perfection. When you are

as good as he is, there are times when it is the only kind of
motivation left.

Except in a very few important team events, such as the
National or World Championships, when you see Ivan float
fishing he will be fishing for a win, or a section win at the very
least. And with his great experience he quickly knows the
potential of the peg he is fishing. If he knows it cannot
produce a good weight, he will quickly lose interest, and this
is one of his great problems. A few years ago on bad days he
would walk the bank and was often criticised for doing so.
Nowadays he tries to work at bad pegs, but it still comes hard
to him. I have met some anglers who have fished beside Ivan
and beaten him – not many, but a few. But what they have
failed to appreciate is that Ivan has been float fishing for a
big weight, whereas they have been concerned only to beat
him. He wants to win the match but all too often they only
want to say they caught more fish than Ivan Marks. If the
big weight tactics fail, naturally someone pimping for a few
pounds weight will have more fish in his net at the end of the
day. But it proves very little. The real test, for Ivan, comes
when he sits next to someone in a situation where each of
them has a chance of winning the match – in other words,
where each is sitting on fish. There are hundreds of also-rans
in the country who will tell you what happens then!

Historically, Ivan's contribution to the development of
float fishing is both interesting and considerable. For the first
half of this century the image of match anglers was of dedi-
cated men with gossamer tackle, Spanish reed rods and
delicate floats pursuing a large quantity of tiny fish. Matchmen were regarded as tiddler-snatchers, their tackle as suitable for not much more than a well-built bleak.

After the Second World War the new generation of
matchmen gradually changed all this. They inherited the
advantages of reliable monofilament line, good fixed-spool

reels and fibreglass rods, and as tackle improved techniques changed. Perhaps it was the invention of the swingtip which ought to be regarded as the biggest single development, but running it a close second was the lead given by match anglers in the use of long-range float fishing using comparatively heavy floats and shotting.

In the sixties anglers from Coventry, led by the famous Billy Lane, and anglers from Leicester led by Ivan Marks, pioneered this new approach, often with great success. It was during this period that Ivan tied his name inseparably to the Zoomer float which he used to such deadly effect on the wide river Welland. Ivan's Welland Zoomer is a float which will take at least 2½ swan shot, plus loading, and that is a far cry from the old pre-war crowquills used on the canals.

Nowadays what were the new kinds of float are well established – antennas and stick floats. But over the years the designs had to be invented and improved, and this is where Ivan has made a great contribution. Before he moved into the tackle business he was already designing and making his own floats, and those prototypes, proved in the heat of competition, have formed the basis for what is now a very big industry, his own range of floats, turned out at the rate of many thousands each week, and sold in tackle shops all over this country and abroad.

Wherever you go to buy floats, you are likely to see some of Ivan's range for sale. Each float is marked with his name and its approximate shot-carrying capacity, and each float is based on a design which he himself uses. At the time of writing he has 26 different kinds of float on the market, comprising, with the different sizes, 142 different floats. Already, millions have been sold.

By my side I have three float boxes neatly laid out with the complete range of Ivan's floats. They are beautifully finished, smart yet practical, and I find it difficult to think of

any freshwater fishing situation in this country which would
demand the use of a float that cannot be found in the Marks
range. I have used all the floats myself and find that,
provided they are used in the correct conditions, they are
excellent.

Ivan's own float box does not bear description! He keeps
most of his prototypes, floats he has made himself, along
with assortments from his commercial range and all sorts of
bits of debris thown in. One day, when he was about to put
on one of his home-made floats, I asked him to use a similar
model from the range he sells. He did so and fished perfectly
with it, but I could tell that he would have been happier with
something he had made with his own hands.

I can think of several top match anglers in the country who
give the impression of being thorough, organised and
efficient. Ivan is the exception. His capacity for apparent
disorder and muddle is legendary. But it is only apparent.
He knows what he wants and what he is doing, but to anyone
else the opposite seems true. Ivan's friend and business
partner, Roy Marlow, tried to warn me. 'When Ivan comes
over tomorrow,' he said to me one day on the phone, 'he'll be
bringing a lot of floats, but watch him! Don't let him get his
hands on them all at once – just give him one at a time.
Otherwise he'll have them all over the place, he'll be breaking
bits off them and you won't know where you are.' He sighed
as if terrible memories were being brought back to him!

How right he was! In less than ten minutes Ivan had more
than 150 floats scattered all over my sitting-room floor. It
was chaos. His small son, Christopher, kept scooping them
up and feeding them to my dog, I was desperately trying to
keep track of what Ivan was saying, his wife, Linda, just sat
there shaking her head sadly, and there, in the middle of it
all, kneeling on floats, talking nineteen to the dozen and
oblivious of everything else was Ivan, absolutely in his ele-

ment. When I expressed concern that I would ever get things organised again, he seemed surprised. 'Don't worry,' he said, 'I can sort 'em all out for you, later. Now, this one –' he snatched a float from the dog and stroked it (the float) lovingly '– I was messing about one day in the shop and I thought . . .' And so it went on. Roy was so right! As for Linda, she seemed like one who has given up all hope of curbing such remarkable eccentricity. I knew how she felt.

I began this chapter by referring to something Ivan said a couple of years ago, that his preference for float fishing is connected with his personality, and when he said that he meant that float fishing was an active, varied way of fishing that held his interest. But there is more to it than that. Float fishing, as opposed to legering, allows Ivan to express his originality – it gives him more scope to open up a gap between himself and other anglers. In all the fascinating combinations of float styles, techniques and skills, Ivan finds an ideal way of being a great individual, an eccentric. Instinctively he realises this.

A few years ago some of Ivan's float-fishing ideas were the subject of some mockery outside his own area, that is the Midlands and East Midlands. There are one or two celebrated cases where he made his critics eat their own words. For example, when he began to pay some visits to stillwater venues in the South of England, his huge antenna floats were much laughed at by locals. But after he had walked off with the top prizes time after time, attitudes suddenly changed. Now, I am told, most people are fishing these venues with huge antenna floats. And he employed similar float-fishing tactics to outfish a field of top matchmen and specimen hunters when *Angling Times* organised a special feature on the catching of huge bream from a Hampshire lake. No one else caught, but Ivan trailed out half a dozen huge bream. Predictably, he insists there was nothing to it.

While this chapter was being written the England team
was in Bulgaria preparing for the World Championship.
Ivan was selected for the fifth consecutive year for this
five-man team event in which eighty of the world's best
match anglers compete for both the team and individual
World Championships. It is by definition a float-fishing
match because legering is not allowed.

England finished a creditable fifth in the team event with
Ivan taking second place in his section. Hours later in the
ninety-minute individual match for World Champion 1976
Ivan became runner-up in a very close finish with the Italian
Dino Bassi. Those are the facts and clearly Ivan Marks put
on a very fine performance indeed. But look behind the bald
facts a little and you will see a lot more.

As most of you will know, the Continental style is speed-
fishing with poles for small fish. It has been generally agreed
that English anglers cannot hope to compete using this style
which the Continentals have perfected over many years. So
English tactics are usually to try for bigger fish with rod and
reel, English style.

In the team match, a three-hour event, Ivan used a rod
and reel. He fished quite close in with a Sarkanda reed float
and caught 251 fish. Only a phenomenal catch of pole-caught
bleak by the Italian Fausto Pasinetti, 615 fish for almost 27
lb, pushed Ivan into second place in his section. But thereby
hangs a tale. In the immediate pre-match practice a mile or
so away, the England team had struggled hard to produce
only a pound or two of fish between them. Then, in the actual
match, the stretch had been teeming with fish. This meant
that the team had to adapt very quickly, in such a short
match, to the situation. Ivan obviously did that.

But consider the second match, the individual contest
shortly afterwards. Knowing there were plenty of fish about,
Ivan, having fished a blinder on the rod and reel, opted then

to fish the pole. Now certainly Ivan has had some experience with the pole, but nothing like that of his Continental opposition. Yet he took on the world's best with a roach pole and came within a mere 3 fish out of 190 of winning the World Championship. Two entirely different float-fishing styles on the same day, both fished in brilliant fashion. That is the kind of versatility that makes Ivan Marks unique in modern match angling, because, with due respect, I would doubt that Dino Bassi could live with Ivan fishing English style. Yet Ivan very nearly pipped him at his own method. And he used one of his own special balsa floats to do it. When I eventually got a telephone line through to Leicester after Ivan returned, I heard him come as near as I have known to congratulating himself. 'Yes,' he said, 'I suppose when you think about it I didn't do too badly.'

This man who finished runner-up on the roach pole is the same man who has float fished his way to victories on the Welland, sometimes with roach, sometimes with bream on the big Zoomer, the same man who has won on the float on the fast-flowing Trent, the swirling Severn, the Warwickshire Avon, the wide Witham, numerous stillwaters, in fact just about everywhere on all kinds of waters both in England and Ireland. It is his versatility which marks him apart, which makes him a hot favourite wherever he fishes, with whatever style. Only recently he finished top individual in the Ladbrokes' Super League, fished on a variety of waters by the country's top anglers.

No man ever had better credentials to write a book on float fishing. Someone once said that the only way to beat Ivan Marks on the float would be to ask for one fish start and be allowed to name the venue. You would then choose to fish in a public swimming baths! There is a lot of truth in that.

But let Ivan take up his own story.

2 The Basics

WHEN MY BOOK on match fishing came out, Peter Collins said a nice thing about it: 'Every angler, not just every match angler, should read it.' I'd like to think that this applies particularly to this book. After all, what does it matter that I'm a match angler? Float fishing is a basic angling technique, and the principles behind it apply to all coarse fishing where a float is being used. Certainly the match anglers go in for what you might call specialist floats, but they can be used by pleasure anglers to their advantage. And the floats I use aren't just for tiddler-snatching: the bigger the fish the better I like 'em!

What are floats for? A daft question, you might think. But what would your answer be? If it's in some way connected with floats registering bites, you're right. But only partly. Floats do other things – they carry your terminal tackle out to where you want to fish, they enable you to fish your bait at different depths and, most important, they determine your bait presentation. If you add up these uses and multiply by the number of possible fishing situations, you'll quickly see that one float, or even a few floats, can never be adequate. On the other hand, you could drive yourself crazy designing a float for every conceivable situation. It's not on. You'd need a lorry to cart them all to your swim. So, do what I do, compromise. Think about the *basic* situations and make sure at least that you're equipped to deal with them.

Basic situations

These are a combination of: flow, width, depth and wind, to put it at its simplest. Let's take the extremes of each. You're fishing a water that's still, narrow, shallow and it's a completely calm day with no ripple at all. What float will you use? Whatever it is, if it works, it will be utterly useless for the opposite extreme – a water that is flowing fast, is wide and deep and you're fishing it in a howling gale. The reverse is true, of course. If you sort out a float for that one it would be quite unsuitable for fishing the first water.

When it's as obvious as this, most people make a fairly sensible decision. I haven't seen too many people fishing a crowquill down the middle of the Severn in the middle of winter, and for that matter I've not often noticed anglers fishing a four swan shot balsa at their rod ends on a canal. The real point, the key to success, is to realise that if a particular float is right for each of the two extremes, then a whole range of floats will be needed to cope with the various combinations of flow, width, depth and wind that come in between.

It's like doing the pools. The permutations are endless. Little wonder then that some anglers settle for having a few little quills for one end of the scale, one or two thumping great floats for the other, and an all-purpose float like a porcupine quill for anything in between. And then you get the perfectionists who have so many floats that they can't remember what half of them are for. That's why I make my own floats. I have a range for each of the basic situations according to my thinking, and that's it.

A situation presents its own problems. The design of a float is determined by what is necessary to overcome those problems. Let's say we're talking about wide stillwaters or slow-moving rivers. The problems here are usually getting your float well out and unaffected by wind or surface skim. The answer is usually an antenna float with its buoyancy at the bottom. Fish it from the bottom only, sink your line and you're some way to being in control of the situation. The deeper the water or the more pronounced the wind, the longer your float. For fishing closer in you will have a more sensitive antenna, perhaps 2 mm, and a float which takes less shot. By using a roach pole I could get down to using a really sensitive float with only a bristle at the tip. With such close control I would fish the float fastened top and bottom.

If the water is flowing I shall look for a float with its buoyancy near the top, perhaps a stick float if the flow is even and the wind gentle. More turbulent flow or a nasty wind demand a sturdier float of a similar pattern, perhaps an Avon or a Balsa. I may, if I want to fish well out in these conditions, use an antenna float with a buoyant antenna, fished bottom only and known as a Waggler. But remember it's always easier to keep control of a trotting float if you fasten it top and bottom.

Control is the key word. That's why you've got to have with you floats which are slight variations on the basic patterns so that you can cope with variations in conditions. Maybe you're fishing a tipped antenna in good conditions on a wide stillwater. Then a wind gets up and the water surface begins to roll and swell. Your tipped antenna is pulled under and you must replace it with one which has more buoyancy in the tip. Or perhaps you're happily trotting a small stick float down a glide quite close in when you find that your fish have begun to move out in the river where it is deeper. Your little stick will hardly cast that far and will not take enough shot to cope with the added depth. So you change it either for a bigger stick or for a float of similar design.

You won't go far wrong if you take bottom only antennas for stillwaters and top and bottom trotting floats for moving waters. The adjustments for depth and wind are then up to you, and you take as your guidelines that increased depth means a heavier float and adverse winds mean bottom only.

If you've got a favourite float, i.e. one that you use for almost every occasion, throw it away. It's no good to you. Your favourite float should vary from day to day and it should be the one that is most suited to existing conditions.

Shotting

There are some anglers who believe that the only use for shot is to cock their floats. They're missing out on an awful lot. Granted that if a novice and an experienced angler were both to shot identical floats down to their tips they would use an identical weight of shot each; still, the critical difference would be where each of them positioned the shot, and how they broke up the total weight into a different number and different sizes of shot. That is what makes the difference because it determines *how your bait is presented to the fish*. And that is what determines whether or not the fish will take it.

I know there are some anglers who have said publicly that they think there is a great deal of nonsense written about shotting, that it's a simple business and greatly exaggerated. But I haven't heard a top match angler say such a thing. Of course it's important, in fact it's absolutely vital. If you're in any doubt, just think of extremes again. A three swan shot float is shotted at ten feet depth by putting all the shot immediately beneath the float. What happens? The bait sinks very gently of its own accord. Then you put all the shot three inches from the hook, and this time the bait sinks to the bottom like a stone. And, never forget this, all the variations in between these two will give a slightly different presentation to the fish. Moving his shot should be a float fisherman's trump card. Discount its importance and you will be a one-style man who catches only on those days when the fish happen to like it your way. Add to the variety offered by shotting, the permutations involved by altering depth and you're right in the middle of some of the finer sophistications of float fishing.

I'm not going into this in depth at this point, but as a basic rule remember that depth and shotting are crucial. There are days when the slight alteration of depth or one single small shot means the difference between a bite a cast and no bite at all. That's a difference that I, at least, can't afford to ignore.

Bites

I wish I'd a pound for every fish I've caught when my float *didn't* go under. I could retire. But when my float does go under it doesn't hang about – it really goes. Why?

First, think always what is happening under the water. If you're fishing a slow-sinking bait, that is without much shot down the line, you'll probably find that fish intercept the bait as it falls. What happens then is that your float, which will settle gradually in the water as each shot sinks, will at some stage fail to settle any further. We call it a bite on the drop, and it can be a deadly way of fishing. Get used to how long it takes your float to cock and then strike at once if it stays too high in the water. Just as good as your float going under, in fact better because it's a quicker way of fishing.

This time your bait has settled on the river bed with maybe one shot resting there as well. Along comes a bream, stands on its head and picks up the bait and with it your last shot. Your float rises in the water by the weight of that shot. A lift bite. Lovely bites, they are! Look out for them.

Now we're trotting our float down a flowing river. Suddenly it stops because a fish has taken the bait without moving off. It's still a bite. It can even happen that a fish will move off with your bait either against the flow or even with it at a slightly faster rate. They're all bites. Hit them. Work on this principle: I know how my float should behave, and if it does anything unusual it's probably because of a fish. Therefore it's a bite. Some days, if you waited for your float to go under you wouldn't strike all day.

But when it does go under it should do so decisively. By that I don't mean fast necessarily, but inevitably. In other words the fish has got the bait and at whatever pace suits it is going to make off with it. If your bites show a lot of dithering and dallying about, something is wrong. Maybe your bait isn't very good, or your hook is too big. It could be that your float isn't suitable for the conditions, or your shotting is wrong. But there will be an answer. Look for it.

When I say this, people sometimes say, 'But how do I know where to start?' Well, think about it. For example, say you are getting bites but can't see them. When you reel in, your bait has been sucked or crushed. Then it's obvious that the bites haven't been registering on your float, so the communication between hook and float isn't working properly. Shorten your depth or put your last shot nearer your hook. If neither works, do both. If you still can't see the bites try a more sensitive float. Do sensible, thoughtful things. Don't just sit and moan. In fact, be grateful there are at least some fish in your swim.

Let's say the reverse is happening. You're getting bites but they're too quick to hit. Then reverse your alterations – add a little more depth and move the bottom shot up a little. Why? Because most probably the fish is feeling that shot and

letting go of the bait before you can strike. Change the float if
necessary to one offering less resistance. The last thing to do
is treat the situation as hopeless and just see how many
unhittable bites you can hit.

These kinds of problem are always kept to a minimum by
the use of small hooks and good, fresh bait. That's why I
always insist on both. Also I aim to feed my fish so that they
become confident, and you must learn how to introduce
loose feed and groundbait. I can't go into that here, but it's
obviously very important.

Lots of anglers seem to have problems with their floats
being towed around but never pulled under. That's usually
because they're fishing miles over-depth, and if you're using
a fragile, succulent bait such as caster you're never going to
catch because the fish will suck the juice from the shell before
you realise what's going on.

What is the best depth? Well, I can't say because it varies
according to the layer of water in which the fish are feeding.
But, as a general rule, fishing just off bottom, perhaps only
by an inch, is the most deadly. Don't take it as a rule, but it's
a good way to start off. If conditions are difficult, though, it
can be tricky to keep a bait presented in this position, and
this is why a good angler with a roach pole can score on
awkward days.

Rods

Obviously you want a suitable rod for the job. In my opinion
for most circumstances a first-class match rod, about thir-
teen feet long, is ideal. You need a tip action for striking and
casting, and you don't want either some floppy thing that
bends in all the wrong places or a stiff affair that breaks you
on the strike. There are several good rods on the market
these days, though I'm sure you'll understand that I feel my

own Persuader model is the best. One word of warning –
they're all fairly expensive.

If you're after particularly hard-fighting fish such as
tench, carp or barbel, you'll need something a bit stronger,
but remember then that you'll have to scale up the rest
of your tackle to match, particularly the line. I always
fish as fine as I can because I'm fishing for bites first and
foremost.

Casting

This has got to be easy. With the right rod and float tackle it
is easy. For an overhead cast with the float fixed bottom only
you should use the action of the rod to send the float across
the water in a high arc. Give the thing some air and never try
to thrash it directly out. If you aim to overcast you can then
check your float at the right point and control its landing so
that the hook, shots and float all land in a straight line. Your
tackle is then fishing for you from the moment it lands. A bad
cast means your float and terminal gear hit the water with a
loud splash and fall into a horrible heap.

An underhand or sideways cast is best for a float fixed top
and bottom. With this arrangement there is always some
danger of a tangle and an underhand cast minimises this. It
also makes for more distance with some kinds of float, especially stick floats.

Tangles can be best avoided by putting a shot directly
underneath the float and then putting the next shot at just
below half depth. This stops the hook back-tangling with the
float during the cast. In any case where the depth is over six
feet I usually place my first shot just below half way simply to
get the bait down more quickly to the fish.

Don't struggle. Use a heavier rig if necessary, because if
you're flailing about, your bait will probably come off on the

cast anyway. Never be afraid of using weight. If it's properly balanced and distributed it doesn't matter.

Choosing a line

No, I don't mean the stuff that goes on your reel. I'm referring to the distance out that you decide to fish. Because usually it pays you to concentrate on one particular line. For a start you will be feeding that line, and if you decide to cast in a different place each time you'll have feed all over the river and you'll never get the fish shoaled up tightly.

How do you decide, because on a big water it could be anywhere from your rod end to forty or fifty yards out? Not an easy one, this, but clearly you mustn't treat it like bingo. I know a lot of anglers who choose their line on a big water by how far they can cast. In a match this can sometimes be right if you're good at long-range float fishing. It means you take the fish out further than the men at the next peg can cast. But it demands two things – one, that you can control your tackle at long range, and two, that there are some fish there to be caught. Most times I am quite happy to let the men near me choose their line and then choose my own, preferably a different one.

The first essential is to find where the fish are. You can then at least catch some, and with any luck you will be able either to hold them there or even to bring them close in. Very often fish will be found feeding on sloping underwater shelves. Look for these by checking depth. Correct feeding is vital if you are to hold your fish and keep them interested in your bait. But remember that you should feed them sparingly until you have searched your swim to establish the most suitable place to shoal up your fish. Novice anglers often tend to throw in a lot of feed as soon as they begin fishing, and usually they throw it in one of two places: either where they think the fish will be, or where they would most prefer to fish, i.e. their favourite line. They thus commit themselves far too early and throw away their chances of catching if conditions are unfavourable to this approach.

If you are pleasure fishing it is usually not difficult to find the best line and keep it producing. But in a match other factors have to be considered, such as the lines chosen by the anglers either side of you. Sometimes you have to fish a line which you would not have selected if you had been pleasure fishing, simply to enable you to keep your fish away from the other anglers. Quite often their tactics can prevent your fishing a line altogether, for example if you intend float fishing for roach a couple of rod-lengths out and the men at the next pegs are groundbaiting heavily and legering for bream.

When, for any one of a number of reasons, you feel you need to change your line, then you may well at some stage soon have to change your float. And this brings me to another basic rule of float fishing.

Never be afraid to experiment

We all had to start fishing sometime. And from our early days most of us will be able to remember how pleased we were when at last we more or less perfected a method and caught lots of fish. The trouble is that many anglers continue throughout their fishing life to cling to one or two well-tried techniques to the exclusion of all others. This kind of conservatism is the kiss of death for a match angler because it stamps him as a one-style, one-water man who will win every now and again when conditions suit his approach. During the long gaps in between his successes he will tell you all about his bad draws and how the fish just wouldn't feed. He will never question his technique. After all, didn't he win a

match a year last August with that very technique? Took
everybody to the cleaners that day. But what he should be
asking himself is why everyone else has been taking him to
the cleaners ever since.

As a float angler what you need, if you will excuse the
fancy word, is a repertoire. You must be able to use a whole
range of techniques because as an angler *you must not expect
always to impose your will on the fish; you must frequently adapt your
technique to what they want.* If you don't accept this, then you
will succeed only when your will coincides with the require-
ments of the fish. In my experience this doesn't happen
often.

Therefore I take the opposite view. I try to be humble. I
see my job as being a constant inquiry into which of many
methods will be the right one for the fish on a particular day.
From my experience I am often able to answer this question
quickly; sometimes I am even right first time. But I am also
often wrong, and then I experiment constantly to find out the
answer. I have often heard match anglers discussing tactics
before a match and declaring quite confidently exactly how
they are going to fish. I can never do this – there are too many
imponderables. Perhaps I can tell you how I shall *start off*,
but that's all.

There is a saying in match fishing that, all things being
equal, the man who is first to find the right method will win
the match. So, every now and again a one-style man will win.
But for consistency of performance over the years he will
come nowhere.

In my case all this comes down to never being satisfied.
When I have perfected a technique I am always looking for
another one. If the fish aren't biting I am always asking
myself why, constantly altering my tackle to try to find out
the answer. If I am catching fish and then the bites suddenly
stop I don't automatically assume that the fish have gone

away, or that they aren't hungry any more. My first reaction
is to feel that the fish *are* still there, and *are* still feeding; but
feeding in a different way. So I change my approach and try to
find out how, by a change of float, or depth, or shotting, or
altering bait presentation, I can begin to catch them again.
Even when you are catching you should not to be too smug:
perhaps you could catch them more quickly, or more easily,
by some slight alteration of tactics.

Float fishing gives me such a range of possible techniques
that I am always confident that some combination or permu-
tation will provide the right answer to a problem. So in my
experience the last thing you should do, if you are not
catching fish, is to carry on in the same way. Quite often the
critical factor will be depth, that is the distance between the
water surface and your baited hook.

Depth

In depth, as in shotting, choice of float and choice of line, too
many anglers are unwilling to change their basic approach.
A common misconception is that the biggest fish always
prefer a bait laid hard on the bottom. This is often true, but
there are so many times when it is not that to fish the one
style only is to miss a lot of sport. Fish feed on the bottom;
they also feed on the surface; and they naturally feed at
various depths in between. It all depends. We can't always
be sure what makes fish decide to feed at a certain depth on a
certain day. Perhaps it is to do with the temperature, or the
flow, or the presence of natural food, sometimes even to do
with the feeding pattern an angler has chosen. For example,
in suitable conditions a good angler, by careful feeding, can
persuade the fish to rise in the water so that he can eventually
catch them on the drop.

The main thing is not to continue fishing at a depth which

is not producing bites. The alteration in depth does not have
to be drastic. A useful tip to remember is that if you have
been catching fish and bites cease, before you change depth
check exactly the depth you have been fishing in case you
want to return to it later. Simply hold the hook beside the
reel on a taut line and mark how many rod rings along your
rod the float is placed. This can save you valuable time in a
match if the fish suddenly decide to return to their original
feeding depth.

A point worth making is that if you change depth simply
by moving your float up or down the line, you will alter your
bait presentation in *two* ways: by fishing at a different depth
and by changing your shot distribution. Although you have
not moved any shots, their position in relation to your float
has changed. In this way you can see how depth and shot-
patterns are interrelated. Therefore you will sometimes
decide to move the position of shots at the same time as you
alter the depth at which the float is fishing.

There are times when the most deadly depth to fish is with
your baited hook a mere inch from the bottom. A bait fished
in this position and gently moved from above by fine control
from an angler using a roach pole can almost be slid into the
mouth of even a reluctant fish. The bait is being manipulated
in front of their very noses. Continental anglers are masters
at this technique, but it cannot be used effectively at long
range or in bad conditions. Very accurate plumbing of the
depth is, of course, essential to this technique.

You can, of course, fish lower than the bottom, that is you
can fish over-depth so that, for example, you are fishing ten
feet deep in seven feet of water. There are times when you
can catch fish like this when no other way will work. It means
that your hook, three feet of line and some shots are all lying
on the river bed. Sometimes in fast water you can make this a
killing method by under-shotting the float to allow for the

drag. The float will, of course, need a buoyant tip and you cannot fish very far out. But it enables you to present a still bait in difficult conditions.

Another situation where it is normal to fish over-depth is when you are running fairly light float tackle, say a stick float or a Waggler, through a fast swim, perhaps on the Trent. If you did not fish over-depth your slight checking of the float as it glides down the swim would cause your bait to rise too high in the water. The easiest guide to just how much over-depth you need to fish to keep your bait near the bottom is to continue increasing depth until the bait catches on the bottom. Then simply move your float an inch or two down the line.

Trotting

The paragraph above describes a typical method of trotting a float down a flowing river. Usually when trotting you will use a float which is attached top and bottom, a float with its buoyancy in the tip. Stick floats and Pacemakers from my own range are good examples of this kind of float.

The trouble with trotting is controlling your float as it moves along. I suggest that the first thing you should do is to perfect the traditional way of doing this, that is by controlling your float in such a way that it is moving without drag at a speed *slightly* slower than that of the current. To achieve this you must be constantly in touch with your float all the time. Some anglers can never quite seem to master this technique.

What are the problems? Well, there are certainly a few, and taken together they account for the mess some anglers find themselves in when trotting. Let's imagine that the float was allowed to travel naturally down the swim. It would quickly reach a point where it was travelling ahead of the

bait. So it must be checked. But the act of checking it, that is
putting a controlled degree of tension between the rod tip
and the float, requires you not only to hold line but to release
some at the same time. Otherwise the float would thrash on
the surface. Therefore the first problem is to perfect the art of
releasing a continuous amount of line which is nevertheless
under control so that although the float is moving down the
swim it is not going too quickly or too slowly. This requires
practice. The line coming off your reel must be fed through
your hand. Different anglers prefer different ways of achieving this, depending often on the kind of reel they are using.
Technically, a centre-pin reel is more suitable for trotting
than an open-faced fixed-spool reel; a closed-face fixed-spool
reel is perhaps the best compromise between the two.

It is worth repeating here a tip I gave in my book on match
fishing, and it concerns the use of a back shot when learning
how to trot correctly. If you put a small shot a few inches
above your float, you can use it as a guide to tell you when to
give more line. If you are checking the line too hard this shot
will lift out of the water, and that is your cue to give line a
little more freely. Without the help of that back shot you
would not have realised you were over-checking until the
float itself had lifted, thus altering your bait presentation.

As you are learning to check your float correctly you will
come across the second problem. The line on the surface of
the water will always be moving faster than your float and it
will, if left, eventually try to overtake it on the inside. This
causes drag, which in turn pulls your float off-line towards
the bank. Down in the water your bait will be pulled
unnaturally across the line of the current. To correct this
result you must constantly 'mend' your line, which means by
use of your rod you lift it off the surface and lay it back in a
straight line behind the float. Beginners find this difficult,
because every time they mend their line they pull their float

off course. It needs a delicate touch. It needs practice, too. The further out you fish the more difficult it is to master these techniques.

Why is it so important to be able to trot a float in this traditional way? There are two reasons. One is that it presents the bait in a way that, more often than not, is the way the fish want it – slightly slower than the speed of the current, ahead of the float and shots, and near the bottom. A good reason, by my reckoning. The other is that having mastered this technique you are then in a position to try variations if the method doesn't work on certain days. Variations include checking the float more severely, thus letting your bait rise higher in the water, checking it in fits and starts so that the bait rises and falls, and hardly checking it at all so that it moves at exactly the speed of the flow.

Normally your shotting will be spaced equally down the line with the smaller shots nearer the hook. But in deep water, apart from a shot under the float, you can put the rest of the shot below half-way, spread out as before. There are numerous examples for you to follow in the next chapter.

A different way of trotting, which has become popular over the last few years, is by using an antenna float, fixed bottom only. Floats used in this way are called Wagglers or Swingers.

The first thing to realise is that you have less control over your float, because if you check it fairly hard it will simply submerge. Also the bait will usually be pulled along behind the float because you cannot control it so well. Basically Waggler fishing gives a quite different bait presentation to traditional trotting, and it is useful for fishing a flowing water fairly well out, or in difficult wind conditions. Waggler experts manage to increase the degree of control they can exert by under-shotting the float so that an inch or more stands out of the water. Technically it seems a crude method compared with the delicate art of stick float trotting, but there are certainly days when it works. That in itself is enough for me.

Long-range float fishing

There's a saying among golf professionals that you 'drive for show and putt for dough', meaning that the spectators tend to think that the big, spectacular drives are what the game is all about but the players themselves realise that the ability to sink the ball over the last few feet is what really wins the money. Other sports have similar catch-phrases. For example, in cricket the spectators love to watch fast bowlers leaping up to the crease and hurling the ball at the batsman; they also like to see the batsman hit the ball right out of the ground. But the players' saying is 'catches win matches'.

Long-range float fishing is perhaps one of angling's most spectacular feats *if it is done well*. Novices are greatly impressed when they see an experienced angler cast his float right across a wide water and then proceed to reel in fish from such distances. But all this needs to be placed in perspective.

First, as a match angler, I am concerned with the business of catching the biggest possible weight of fish within the time of the match. Because I am technically capable of float fishing at extreme range I will do so gladly if I think I can catch more fish by that method. But this does not happen all that often, and certainly not as frequently as many people think. Over the years my name has become associated with the use of heavy floats and long-distance fishing: the use of the Zoomer on the Welland is a typical example. And it is quite true that I have had a lot of success with this method. But it is also true that I have won a lot of matches by float fishing at moderate or even close range and I certainly don't fish the far bank unless I have carefully calculated the odds.

The odds go something like this. They are in my favour if the fish are a long way out, or if float fishing is likely to be more effective than legering. They are also in my favour if the fish out there are likely to be bigger than the fish close in, say bream as opposed to roach. But on many days the odds are against me. If fish can be caught more successfully close in, I must lose. Even if they can be caught equally easily close in, I shall lose because close-in fishing is faster fishing.

The point is that if I, who can fish efficiently at long range, find it of only limited use, then many others who cannot do it properly should approach the whole technique cautiously. There are many difficulties.

Getting the float out there is one thing. Controlling it and recognising bites is another. Feeding correctly at extreme range is harder still. One way of understanding the technical problems of long-range float fishing is to see that it magnifies alarmingly any weaknesses in your ordinary float fishing. Look at it this way. If, fishing a couple of rod lengths out, you find it difficult to cast accurately, how are you going to manage at forty yards plus? If at ten yards you have difficulty in seeing slight lifts and nudges of your float, what will you be able to see at four times the distance? Do you occasionally get tangles during the cast? Then how many will you get at extreme range? Can you feed accurately onto an area of water the size of a tea plate at ten yards? If not, how big an area will you need at forty? Something about the size of a dance floor, I should imagine.

Range magnifies weaknesses in technique, and so the lesson should be obvious. But to many anglers it isn't, and you can see them trying vainly to fish at long range when they haven't even mastered the business of fishing at their rod end. They would catch more fish, and finish up better-tempered, if they fished sensibly within their limitations. I am sure that these people feel that long-range float fishing is somehow a proof of ability; but in most cases it is a proof of the exact opposite. A method must be judged by its results, and it is only in the hands of an expert that this technique can produce a good weight of fish.

All right, you may say, then tell me how I can become an expert! Well, for a start you have no chance if your eyesight is poor. You need really good eyesight or you will just not be able to see the bites. Watching a float tip among ripples at long range is very tiring on your eyes if you do it with full concentration for any length of time. Some people find it gives them headaches, and for others after an hour or so the effect of light and ripple causes them to have optical illusions so that the float seems to disappear when in fact it hasn't moved at all. There is the perfectly true story of the match angler who spent a full five hours float fishing way out. He was so tired when he got home that after tea he fell asleep on the settee, holding his wife's hand while she watched the television. Even though his eyes were closed he could still see his float riding across the water. All of a sudden it disappeared, he struck mightily and woke up to find that he had thrown his poor wife clean across the settee and onto the carpet! So let that be a warning to you!

However, let's suppose you have good eyesight. The next step is to make sure that you are perfectly competent at float fishing at normal distances. Remember that this includes the ability to feed accurately. When you begin to try to increase your range, do so gradually. That way you are likely to see what is going wrong. Casting must be smooth and not snatched, and you should aim the float at a point high above where you want it to land. Allow it to describe a high, looping trajectory, and check it as it lands by feathering the line with your finger. It is always best to overcast rather than undercast as you can easily pull the float back towards you.

Properly cast, the hook, shots and float should land lightly on the surface in a straight line at right angles to the bank.

The float, of the antenna or Missile type, should carry enough shot for you to be able to cast it the required distance without effort. Even at long range you must be in full control of things. The equivalent of at least two swan shot needs either to be built into the float or placed immediately beneath it. If you are locking your float onto the line with shot, it is a good idea to put a short length of silicone or valve rubber tubing between each shot and the float ring. This cushions the impact of both casting and striking.

The things required to achieve distance are: a reel spool almost full of the finest practical breaking strain line (say, between 2 and 3 lb); correct casting action; a float with a heavy enough shot-carrying capacity; and a float which is well balanced, that is one which flies through the air like a dart and does not waggle about.

The surest way of avoiding back-tangles during the cast is to make sure the first shots on the line, apart from the ones directly beneath the float, are just below half-way between float and hook. If you regard all succeeding shots lower down as hinges for back-tangles, you can place them in the best positions by making sure at each point that the hook, if hinged back at each shot, cannot reach the one above it.

The Zoomer is a float which needs to be cast underarm and attached top and bottom. The tangling possibilities are greatly increased by this, and therefore you should note that the shot-pattern for this float cannot have much variation. It should only be used in ideal conditions.

A further factor which frequently makes long-distance float fishing difficult is wind and drag. If the wind is really bad there is little point in trying this technique. But a moderate wind, particularly from the right or left, can be overcome more easily if you cast across and into it rather than across and with it. You will get far fewer back-tangles this way, though a number of people tend to think that the opposite is the case.

Drag or surface skim is a great nuisance, and you can only avoid it by overcasting and sinking your line. Lines washed in detergent sink well, but they deteriorate quickly. Certain makes of line have a tendency either to float or sink more easily than others, and this is something that you should bear in mind when choosing a particular line for a particular job.

A lot of anglers find that when they strike at long-range bites they only prick the fish – it is on for a moment, then gone. This is caused either by using hooks that are too big or by not striking hard enough. At forty yards range, with a correctly balanced rod and line, the suppleness of the rod and the elasticity of the monofilament line should allow you to strike heftily into a brick wall without fear of breaking. The secret is to strike powerfully, but with control.

Interchangeable float caps are useful for this kind of fishing. If you have a range of colours, say red, orange, black and white, you are in a position to alter the colour of your float tip in a matter of seconds. A simple change from sunny conditions to dull, or to shifting light caused by moving clouds, can often make your original choice of float tip unsuitable. Be prepared.

And of course there is the question of accuracy. Being able to cast the distance, and feed accurately at that distance, is all made pointless if you cannot put the float in exactly the same area as your feed *time after time*. You will find that a really top-class angler will be able to put his feed and his float into an area not much bigger than a dustbin lid even at extreme range.

This all requires practice. But if you succeed in mastering the technique it will enable you to catch more fish on *some*

days than anyone else. The real art, once you know *how* to do
it, is to know *when* to do it. That can only come from experience, but a good working rule to begin with is not to attempt
long-range float fishing in bad weather conditions.

Balance

Take a dozen floats which all look identical, fish with each in
turn and you will find that in practice they don't all perform
in quite the same way. I can tell, instinctively, when a float is
'right'. It depends, of course, what kind of float it is and what
it is intended to do. For example, a trotting float which is not
quite 'right' will somehow fail to go through the swim in
quite the way you want it to. Either it will not ride properly,
or it will not register the final shot sensitively. Perhaps it is
too easily disturbed when the line is mended. It could be any
one of a dozen little things which prevent it from being
perfect. All I know is that when a float is 'right' I can tell at
once. No doubt it comes from years of experience.

When I make floats I make a number of each kind, and
usually I throw a lot of them away; sometimes all of them.
Each design of float has its own kind of balance, the relationship between length, volume and density of the various
materials. Because materials vary, however marginally, it is
next to impossible to produce two floats that will be identical
in performance.

Earlier I said that if you have a favourite float you should
get rid of it. In that context I meant you ought not to use one
float for several fishing conditions. But certainly when you
find a float that is 'right' you should keep it for use in the
conditions for which it has been designed. Be a perfectionist;
it is difficult enough at times to catch fish without handicap-
ping yourself by using an essential piece of equipment which
is less than perfect.

Weight

Never be afraid of using floats with a heavy shot-carrying capacity if you feel that conditions demand the use of such a float. Floats do not just register bites; they enable you to control your tackle and they enable you to present the bait correctly to the fish. Wind, depth and flow in various degrees frequently produce conditions where the use of lead is *essential* to success.

I'm no scientist, and I don't want to get involved in all the arguments about volume and density, water displacement, inertia and all the rest. It doesn't interest me. If a scientist can prove on paper that a heavy rig is less sensitive than a light one, then let him prove it on the river bank in fishing conditions that demand the use of lead. For me, if a method produces, it's right. I like to do my sums while I'm fishing. When I'm catching steadily on a three swan shot antenna while people round me are struggling on lighter gear, I feel I've worked out the answer to my own satisfaction.

If conditions are absolutely ideal things would of course be different. But conditions hardly ever are and almost always the only practical way to overcome them is by using lead. Naturally there is no point in using more than is necessary, but neither is there any point in using less.

Real situations can make nonsense of theory. For example, you may be fishing a river on a day of absolute calm. All you want to do is catch roach off your rod end at a depth of six feet. There is no flow. How much shot would you need? In theory, very little. In practice you could need to use a float taking two or three swan shot. Because if there were shoals of bleak around, you would never get your bait down to the roach if you used a delicate rig. I have known times when even two swan shot inches from the hook was not enough to get the bait through the bleak quickly enough. No, I'm not much of a one for theories.

Having said all this, I agree that using lead requires some skill. The float balance and shot distribution must be right so that the combination is as sensitive as possible. The point is that if, by using weight, you can get the bait to the fish in the right way, you stand a much better chance of catching than someone whose rig is beautifully light, offers hardly any resistance, but fails to present the bait properly.

Really, I try not to be too dogmatic about anything. I'm all for using weight, but only in the right circumstances. I suppose I have done as much as anyone during the last twenty years to popularise the use of lead in float fishing. Yet I'm probably as well known for my exploits with a match-stick and no shots at all as I am for taking bream from the far bank of the Welland with the big Zoomer.

Knowing your floats

We always have to come back to this in the end. It's the basis of everything in float fishing. The worth of a float has nothing to do with its size, or colour, or attractiveness. It depends entirely on how well it does its job, and it is up to the angler to know exactly what that job is. If you believe that one float is as good as another, and that it's the skill of the angler that matters, you're wrong. And if you believe that one float is as good as another and everything depends on whether the fish want to bite, you're just as wrong.

In the next chapter I'm going to tell you all about the floats that I use, why I use them and exactly how I use them. This knowledge, second nature to me now, is the basis of my success. I hope that you, too, will find it invaluable.

3 My Floats and How I Fish Them

THIS IS GOING to be the most technical part of my book and I hope you will try to follow it carefully and learn from it. By this stage you should be convinced that much of the art of float fishing lies in being able to choose the correct float for each situation. Here I hope to tell you all about my own range of floats and the situations for which they were designed.

In a way I'm lucky because all my original designs are now commercially produced in thousands and are used by anglers all over the country, and abroad. Each of my floats has my name on it and also the approximate shot capacity. A word of warning here – the shot numbering on a float simply tells you in the simplest terms the *total weight* of shot which will cock the float properly. *It does not mean that you should use those actual shots when fishing the float*. For example, if a float is marked as carrying three swan shot, you are not being told to take three swan shot from your box and fasten them somewhere on the line. This would give a very crude set-up. What you will do is break down the shot load of three swan into smaller shots, e.g. 1 swan, 1AAA, 2BB, 2 No. 1, 3 No. 4, 2 No. 8, and one or two very small shot for final adjustment. In effect you will make up a combination of shots to suit the conditions you are fishing under, and my shot capacity on the float will simply guide you as to how much total weight the float will hold.

It is easier to assess this total weight when using various shots if you have some idea of the relative weights of the various sizes. Unfortunately the numbering of shots is related to the sizes of shot in cartridges, and it so happens that the relative weights are seldom exact. But, roughly speaking, you can expect that:

2 AAA	=	1 Swan shot
2 BB	=	1 AAA
3 No. 1	=	1 AAA
4 No. 4	=	1 BB
7 No. 8	=	1 BB
20 No. 12	=	1 BB

From these you can make some comparative figures yourself, bearing in mind that the full range of shots is as follows:

SSG (Swan shot) – SG – AAA – BB
No. 1, 2, 3, 4, 5, 6, 7, 8, 9, 10, 11, 12 and 13.

Really, there is too great a range here, particularly for beginners, and I myself do not use all of the numbered shot: my own range is SSG – SG – AAA – BB – No. 1, 4, 6, 8, 10, 11, 12, 13. The very smallest shots, dust and micro-dust, are invaluable for making the final, sensitive adjustments to bait presentation.

Working shot

When you look at the shotting diagrams in this section you will see that invariably the last few feet of the terminal tackle consists of *small clusters of small shot* – e.g. 4 No. 1, 3 No. 4, 2 No. 6, followed by 1 No. 8. You may wonder why each

cluster is not replaced by a single shot of a larger size. The
answer to this is crucial: the clusters of shot, what I call the
working shot, are there so that the bait presentation can be
altered by sliding shot from one cluster to another. I could
alter the above pattern in a number of ways – e.g. by moving
down to the 3 No. 4 shot any or all of the 4 No. 1 above; or by
moving down any or all of the 3 No. 4 to the 2 No. 6 below.
All the permutations over the last few feet give me endless
flexibility in changing presentation, whereas if each cluster
was a single shot the possible variations would be severely
reduced. An understanding of this principle is vital if you are
to benefit fully from the information in this section.

 Two other points follow in connection with the idea of
working shot. First, the shot must be soft or it will not move
easily along the line and will damage it. Second, all the shot
diagrams you see are not hard-and-fast; they simply suggest
a sensible way of beginning to fish with a particular float.
Final adjustments are up to the individual angler fishing a
particular swim.

Categorising floats

This can be a dangerous thing to do if you are discussing
more than two dozen different designs, as I am about to do.
For example, if you divide floats into those fished top and
bottom, and those fished bottom only, where do you place
Balsas and Pacemakers, which can be fished either way?

I have decided to make two basic categories, floats for
running waters, and floats for still and slow-moving waters. I
shall try for each category to begin with floats which are for
the easiest conditions and work through them gradually to
the ones most suitable for the most difficult conditions, e.g.
extreme range, depth, flow or wind. I hope this approach
will impose some pattern and sense on what can be a difficult

and confusing subject. The only float which clearly can be effective on both running and still waters is the Waggler and I shall deal with it separately.

In a way it is fortunate that my float business is well-established, so that it cannot be thought that in some way I could be using this section as a shop window to sell my floats to the public. There are already several million of my floats in use everywhere, and I hope that anyone reading what follows will be helped to use these floats efficiently. They are what I use myself, and there is no guarantee I can give you greater than that!

Part One : Floats for Running Waters

It should be obvious that if a float is going to perform satisfactorily in flowing water it must have in its design a built-in resistance to some of the adverse effects of running water, e.g. drag, turbulence, boil. The conventional trotting floats have most of their buoyancy near the tip, e.g. stick floats and Avons. The unconventional floats used for trotting, or rather reverse trotting, do not have their buoyancy near the tip, e.g. Duckers and Swingers. Even so, the tip of any trotting float needs to be made of a fairly buoyant material so that it is not easily pulled under.

My range of trotting floats, excluding Wagglers, covers eight different kinds and a total of sixty floats. We begin with a stick float taking 3 No. 6 shot and end with a 3½ swan shot Balsa.

The Stick Float

Specifications: The stick float is a man-made version of the natural crowquill. Its unique feature is its balance which is achieved by a combination of cane and balsa. The cane forms the base and balsa the tip. When the two materials are joined in perfect proportion the float will cast, cock and trot perfectly. More of this later.

I have a range of twelve sticks, the largest taking 5 AAA shot and the smallest 3 No. 6.

Use: Of all the floats, except possibly the Zoomer, the stick is the one that can only be used effectively in strictly defined conditions. Really, it is a strange float because it can be one of the most deadly, or useless, floats depending on how and where you use it.

Its special balance means that it can give a particular kind of bait presentation which is very effective for catching roach, dace or chub. To get this presentation you must:

a) fish it in the correct conditions;
b) cast it correctly;
c) shot it correctly;
d) fish at a particular depth.

Ignore the basics and you would be better off fishing with a wooden clothes peg.

First, the correct conditions. These concern depth, power of flow, distance and wind. The depth must not be excessive – anything over eight feet is pushing towards the limit, and four to six feet is ideal. The flow must be even and not excessive. You don't want a rough, boily swim for stick float work. Also, the stick is not a long-range float, in fact it's at its best close in. Finally, it should never be fished in heavy or downstream winds.

So, fish your stick in the right conditions and you have one of the best floats in the business. Try to make it work when one of the above factors is against you and you'll begin to wonder why people have such a high regard for this float.

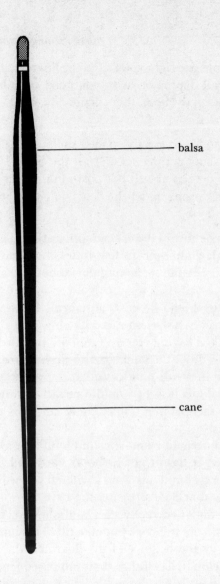

balsa

cane

Figure 1 Stick float

If conditions are right you fasten the float top and bottom, *always*. For all depths of swim you need your biggest shot directly beneath the float; then, depending on the depth, you shot as follows:

> 6 feet and less: evenly spaced shots all the way down, the shots getting smaller all the time.
>
> Over 6 feet: as above, but position the first shot (apart from the one under the float) half-way between float and hook.

You will not be sure of the exact depth until you have put the float through your swim a few times, but once you have found it you should set your float about six inches over-depth.

Stick floats should be cast underarm. I know that most anglers always cast overarm, but if you want to get the best out of stick float fishing you really should practise the underarm cast. It allows the stick float to flight across the water like a dart, it prevents tangles and, most important, it lands your terminal tackle lightly on the surface in a straight line. The float is then fishing immediately, and this is one of its great virtues.

All these instructions must sound a bit alarming. Surely, you may say, it hasn't got to be as hard-and-fast as this. Well, I'm sorry, but it has. And I will tell you why. It's all to do with how that float presents the bait.

When it lands, correctly cast and shotted, it will cock immediately – not full cock but on a tilt. This initial cocking is achieved by the balance of the float and the single shot directly beneath it. The other shots fall in sequence, giving a classic situation for you to get bites on the drop. The shot pattern means that the hook is always in direct contact with the float so that a bite will register at any depth from the surface to the bottom. This is why the stick float is so deadly

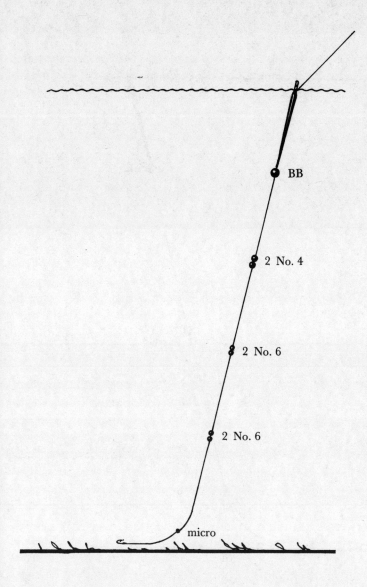

BB

2 No. 4

2 No. 6

2 No. 6

micro

Figure 2   Basic shotting pattern for a stick float fished at a depth
of less than 6 feet

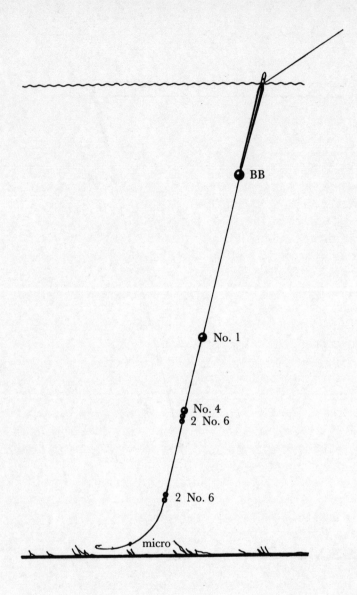

BB

No. 1

No. 4
2 No. 6

2 No. 6

micro

Figure 3   Basic shotting pattern for a stick float fished at a depth
of over 6 feet

when casters are being used as bait, a) because the fish cannot suck or 'shell' the caster without the float registering a bite, and b) because loose-feed casters in flowing water will often encourage roach to rise in the water to intercept the feed, thus giving bites on the drop.

If you are not getting bites on the drop you are still in a perfect situation for trotting the bait through your swim. Because you are fishing over-depth you will be forced to check your float slightly, and this will cause your bait to travel ahead of the float, fluttering enticingly above the bottom as you hold back, dropping back again as you slacken tension. If you check too hard you will soon know because your stick will lift almost out of the water. Get it right and you can just about do anything you like with the float and bait.

But it's a delicate style. Downstream winds and rough water mean the float won't cast and work properly. Almost any other float would give you better presentation then, and you are abusing your stick float. Just picture to yourself the ideal swim: a calm day, just a light breeze pushing gently upstream, a steady even glide five or six feet deep, perhaps a gravel bottom, no snags, no turbulence, a shoal of hungry roach – the mind boggles! A stick man's Paradise. It's an unbeatable float *on its day*.

There are a few other points worth bearing in mind if you're a perfectionist. Don't use stick floats in still water; don't use them attached bottom only; use long ones for deep water or fishing three or four rod lengths out; use shorter ones for shallow water or fishing close in; shot them well down and hold them back; don't fish them laid on.

Incidentally, if your stick doesn't cast or cock properly, get rid of it. If the balance is wrong, you'll never work it as I've described. A good stick is beyond price; a bad one is just a nuisance!

The Carrot

Specifications: Carrots are relatively small floats with a balsa body tapering upwards to a broad shoulder. The tip is an insert of 2 mm cane, and the effect is to combine something of the sturdiness of a balsa float with the bite-registering sensitivity of an antenna. In appearance Carrots are like inverted Arrows, floats which I shall be describing later.

I have a range of four, carrying 5 BB down to 2 BB. There is no need for a Carrot in excess of 5 BB as its function can then be more efficiently carried out by another kind of float.

Use: For me, Carrots are scratchers. I class them in the same category as Darts that I use on stillwaters. This is not to belittle them in any way, but quite honestly I wouldn't expect to win a big match on running water with a Carrot, unless conditions were exceptional. Carrots are designed to register shy bites, and certainly I have found I can catch on a Carrot when other floats have failed. But when these conditions prevail it is really a question of scratching for ounces rather than thumping out a match-winning weight. They are ideal for winning gruelling sections, or fighting for precious points in a team match.

The floats work like this. The balsa body provides stability and the fine cane tip provides sensitivity. But, like the stick, the Carrot cannot cope in adverse conditions. The tip is so sensitive that heavy flow, uneven flow, turbulence or bad winds cause it to register false bites. Also, the maximum shot capacity of 5 BB means that it cannot be fished at distance or in deep swims.

In many ways the Carrot is happiest in the same conditions as the stick, but whereas the stick is miles ahead when the fish are feeding well, the Carrot has the edge when the

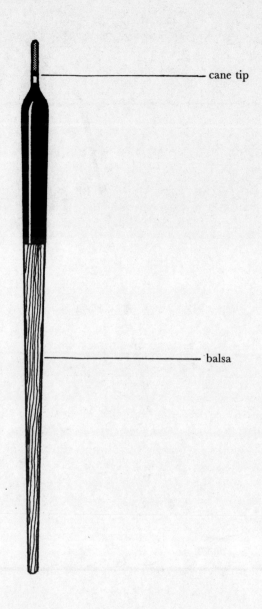

cane tip

balsa

Figure 4 Carrot

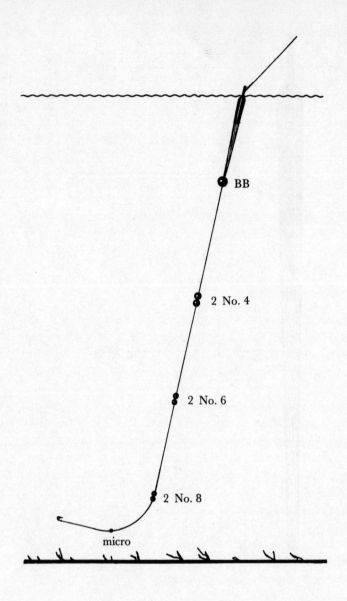

Figure 5   Basic shotting for a Carrot fished at a depth of less than
            6 feet

going is hard. At these times it has three distinct advantages over the stick:

a) the tapered balsa body gives the float a stability which eliminates false bites;
b) the fine tip can be submerged by the fish with the minimum of resistance;
c) the Carrot will, in good conditions, register lift bites.

In fair conditions, fishing not too far out in not too deep water, sticks and Carrots between them should enable you to catch fish. The stick is for good days, the Carrot for bad.

The Pacemaker

Specifications: There is a logical connection between this float and the first two, particularly the stick. Pacemakers are designed to do much the same job as sticks, *but under more difficult conditions*. The materials used are still balsa and cane, but the shape and proportions are different.

The balsa body is sturdier than that of the stick so that its appearance is fatter. Even so, at its widest point the body begins to taper down most elegantly towards the tip, and this gradual shoulder plays an important part in the float's performance. The balsa is of a higher density than that used in the stick, so that it is slightly heavier for its volume and takes less shot. This helps the float to ride more smoothly in rough conditions.

The cane insert at the bottom is very short compared with that of a stick, not much more than an inch. This, together with the high-density balsa and the sturdier shape, gives the Pacemaker that extra stability over the stick.

I have a range of six, each shorter than the last and with a shot capacity from 5 AAA to 3 BB.

Use: Consider the limitations of the stick that I listed earlier. Then, as a rough working guide, tell yourself that when conditions become unsuitable for the stick it is time to put on a Pacemaker.

It works something like this: if the water is a little too deep for a stick, a Pacemaker will work; if the flow is too fast or turbulent for a stick, a Pacemaker will cope; if the wind is making problems for your stick float, a Pacemaker will behave better. What it allows you to do is get something close to stick float bait presentation in conditions where a stick float couldn't be used effectively.

Don't however, take this to ridiculous extremes. A Pacemaker won't work miracles, and I'm *not* telling you to fish one in fifteen feet of boiling, racing water in a downstream gale. Come to think of it, I wouldn't advise you to use *any* float in those conditions. No, you just treat your Pacemaker as an extension to your stick float so that you can cope with slightly rougher conditions.

I originally designed the Pacemaker for fishing the river Blackwater in Ireland, and I tried to produce a float which would give good bait presentation in fairly deep, fairly fast water. Since I invented it I have been very pleased with its performance. Apart from its basic function, which I have just described, it has some extra qualities which both I and many more anglers have found extremely useful on a variety of flowing rivers in this country.

For a start, the Pacemaker is a very adaptable float. The shorter ones can be used on fairly fast waters like the Trent and the larger ones can cope with the depth and turbulence of rivers like the Wye or the Severn. The float can be fished bottom only, but this is not to be recommended. In a reasonable downstream wind you can still fish a Pacemaker top and bottom. By fishing it bottom only you are depriving it of one of its great attributes – its response to control by the angler.

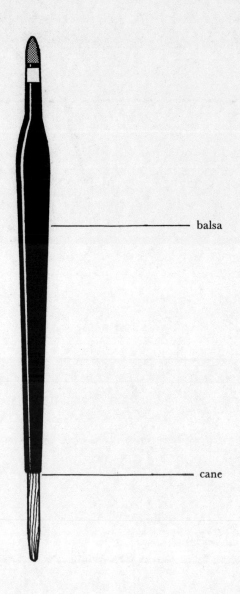

balsa

cane

Figure 6   Pacemaker

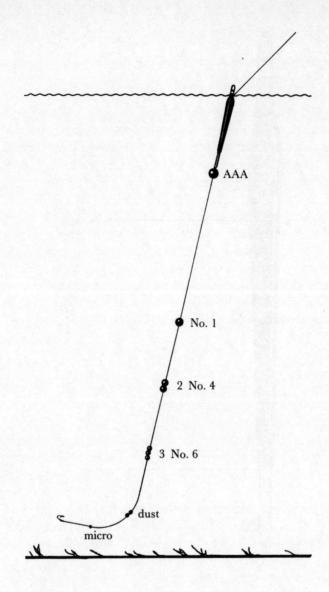

Figure 7   Basic shotting for a Pacemaker

Check a stick fairly sharply toward the end of a long trot and it will come out of the water. But a Pacemaker, because of its stability and the pressure of water on its sloping shoulder, will not. You can control its pace at will as it moves through your swim – hence its name – and this in turn means you can control your bait presentation. That's what I like!

It should be obvious that the average shot pattern on a Pacemaker will need to be slightly heavier downstairs to beat flow and depth, heavier, that is, than you would hope to use with a stick. All things considered, it is one of my favourite trotting floats, combining stability with sensitivity. Slightly undershotted it will glide smoothly through quite rough water. With the sturdiness of a balsa and the sensitivity of a stick it can, on its day, give you the best of both worlds. And that is something I like to have, if I can!

The Avon

Specifications: This popular, all-purpose trotting float has traditionally been made with a cane stem and a balsa body placed towards the top of the float.

My Avons are, in my opinion, superior to the conventional design because the body *and tip* are constructed from a single piece of balsa. This unit is joined at the base to the usual cane stem.

The increased buoyancy of the balsa tip, as opposed to cane, enables the float to ride rough water without being pushed off course. The tip is reasonably fine which means that it will register shy bites sensitively.

I have a range of six Avons, from 5 AAA shot capacity down to 3 BB.

Use: One of the reasons why Avon floats are so popular is

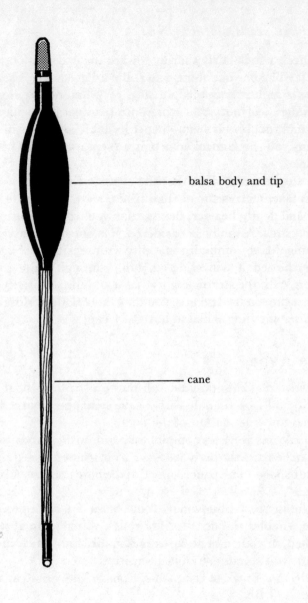

balsa body and tip

cane

Figure 8   Avon

that provided you have a range of sizes you can use them to good effect on just about any running water. In this sense they are not a specialist float in the way that, say, a stick is. If all you had in the way of floats was a set of sticks, there would be many occasions when you would be beaten. But a set of Avons will help you to catch anywhere where the water is moving.

Of course, this does not mean that Avons make all other running water floats redundant. Far from it. When conditions are right for a specialist float it will likely produce more fish than an Avon. It's a question of deciding which float is most suitable, and if you're not sure, then you can rely on an Avon to give a reasonable performance.

The reason for the Avon's suitability for almost all trotting situations lies in its design. It has the classic features of a trotting float – buoyancy high up, sturdiness with streamlining, and stability. Naturally it performs best in ideal conditions – that is, with an upstream wind and moderate, even flow. It should, of course, be attached top and bottom and fished in the traditional trotting style.

However, it is a versatile float and will cope with conditions that are not favourable. The larger floats, with a more streamlined body and heavy shot-carrying capacity, can be fished well out in quite deep and fast-moving water. Yet the smaller ones will perform well close-in in shallow, gliding swims. Avons can even be fished as Wagglers, attached bottom only, but this is wasting the best features of their design. If conditions are so bad that none of the Avon range can cope fished top and bottom, you would be advised to change to a different kind of float.

Avons can be shotted according to conditions in the same way as Pacemakers.

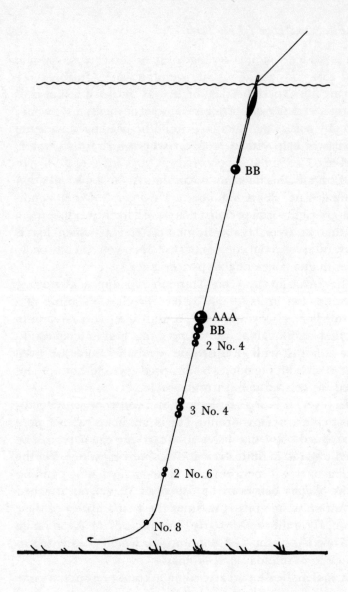

BB

AAA
BB
2 No. 4

3 No. 4

2 No. 6

No. 8

Figure 9   An Avon float shotted to fish a fairly deep and
turbulent water

The Balsa Float

Specifications: As its name implies, the Balsa float is constructed entirely of balsa, and because this is one of the lightest materials, it follows that the float will ride the roughest water without constantly being dragged under. They are also able to carry a heavy shot-load for their size and this means that the bait can be fished deep even in a strong flow.

My Balsas are fairly stubby in shape and the slope of the shoulder towards the tip helps to keep the float down in the water even when it is being held back against a powerful current. The range of sizes is considerable – eleven in all, ranging from the huge 7 AAA size down to a tiny float taking only 3 No. 4 shot.

Use: I think it's fair to say that you wouldn't often *choose* to fish a Balsa rather than another float, it's just that conditions sometimes don't give you any say in the matter. Three factors determine whether you will need to use the big Balsas – rough water, powerful flow and depth. Big Balsas will help you to ride the rough water and still keep control, and their stability and shot-capacity will mean that you can get your bait down to the fish even in deep or powerfully flowing water.

The biggest Balsas are most suitable for fishing big baits like bread, wasp grubs and luncheon meat. The movement of the bait in the flow does not register as a bite. Small baits fished with these big floats do not give good bite registration and I would not advise you to use single maggots or casters. Wherever possible the floats should be fished top and bottom, and although they can't be fished properly at extreme range they do perform well at considerable distances such as the middle of the river Severn.

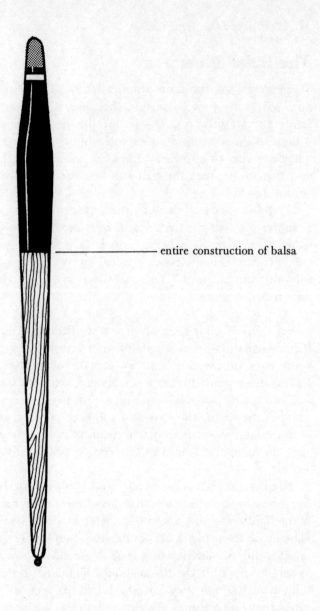

entire construction of balsa

Figure 10 Balsa

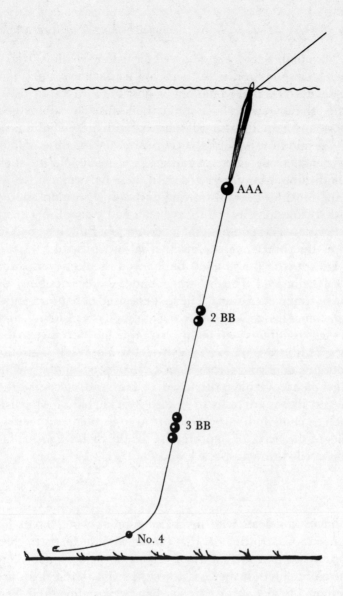

Figure 11   A Balsa float shotted to fish a fast turbulent water

The small Balsas are designed for fishing shallow, tricky swims close-in, and with them you can achieve good bait presentation which would not be possible with a stick float. Often shallow swims have surface boil caused by submerged rocks, and a small Balsa will cope well with these conditions.

The middle range of Balsas is ideal for fishing three or four rod lengths out where conditions are unsuitable for stick float fishing. Many anglers regard these particular floats as being ideal for general trotting purposes. I wouldn't agree with this because as you'll have realised by now I'm a great believer in a certain float for a certain job. Still, it's good to know that other anglers find the Balsas so useful.

Except with the smallest Balsas, you should never worry about using lead. They're strong, buoyant floats designed for use in rough conditions. The first essential of bait presentation comes a long way before the question of sensitivity, and in such conditions your main job is to get the bait down to the fish. This means that you may well use more shot along the bottom half of your terminal tackle than you would use with other floats we have discussed so far. And of course the biggest Balsas are likely to be used with big baits for big fish such as chub and barbel. Bites tend to be bold and there is seldom the need, or opportunity, for the delicate presentation needed to tempt roach and dace.

I have now dealt with my basic running-water floats for conventional trotting. By that I mean with the float attached top and bottom so that, usually, it can be held back to allow the bait to precede the float down the swim. These floats are designed to give this particular bait presentation, and their limitations are that bad conditions, most especially downstream winds, can prevent their being used effectively.

We therefore come to the 'other' kind of trotting floats, those which are designed either to achieve reasonable bait presentation in bad conditions, or to give a deliberately different bait presentation, known as reverse trotting. It is really up to the angler, by the way he fishes these floats, to decide whether he will do his best to imitate traditional bait presentation, or whether he will aim for reverse trotting. The three kinds of float are all capable of being used in either way.

The Swinger Float

At first sight you may not be able to distinguish a Swinger from any other kind of antenna float, but if you had a set of each the differences should be clear.

Specifications: Swingers have a streamlined body at the bottom of the float and a Sarkanda reed antenna. I have two ranges, a set of four and a set of five, and what makes them different to all the other kinds of antenna is that in each range the size and shape of the bodies are identical and it is only the length of antenna that varies.

If you take any other sets of antenna floats you will see that the body increases in size in relation to the length of the tip. Therefore the shot-carrying capacity of the floats increases according to their overall length. Swingers are the exception. In my range of four the longest Swinger has a 9 inch antenna and the shortest a 6 inch antenna. Yet the shot difference is only from 4 AAA to 3 AAA. And in my second range of five floats there is virtually no difference in shot-carrying capacity – each float takes approximately 3 AAA.

Therefore the important design feature of my Swingers is not so much the construction of the individual float as the

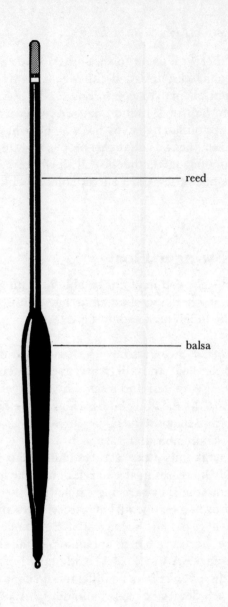

reed

balsa

Figure 12(a)   Swinger – Set 1

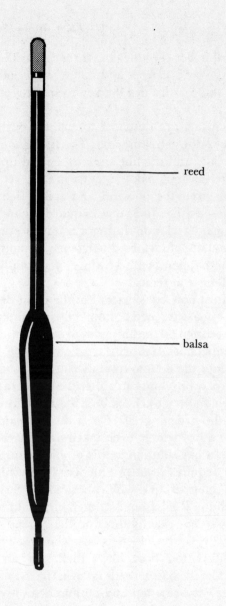

reed

balsa

Figure 12(b)   Swinger – Set 2

relationship between the floats in each set. The critical factor within the set is length and not a variety of shot-capacity. And in this feature lies the key to the use of the Swinger.

Use: Swingers are designed to enable you to fish running water in a downstream wind. The float should be attached bottom only and the line sunk to the rod tip after the cast. The different lengths of antenna in each set are to combat different strengths of wind and skim. Because the shot-capacities are the same you can quickly change floats if wind conditions deteriorate during a fishing session. With other floats, you are often forced to change to another *kind* of float when this happens; with a Swinger you simply change to one with a longer antenna.

We must now consider one of the great disadvantages of fishing a float attached bottom only in running water: when you put tension on the line to try to control the float, it simply disappears beneath the surface. So you have a real problem. If you leave the float to trot downstream as it likes you have no control over it and can't alter the presentation of the bait; yet when you try to check it, it registers false bites. You've beaten the dragging effect of a downstream wind, but in order to do so you've been taken over by the float.

There is one solution to this problem, but it's not all that easy. It requires a lot of practice. Really, there aren't too many anglers around who can handle a Swinger with real skill. Johnny Rolfe from Nottingham would be an example, but they're not exactly thick on the ground.

Basically, your problem is this: when you are trotting with a top-and-bottom float, like a stick, you can hold back the float and let the bait precede it down the swim. Now the wind won't let you use a top-and-bottom float, and the Swinger, attached bottom only to beat that wind, won't let you hold it back! It looks like stalemate, and a lot of anglers just hope the

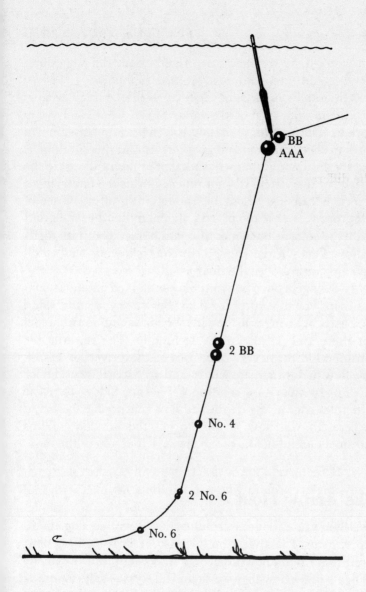

Figure 13 Typical shotting for a Swinger float

fish won't mind the new bait presentation. But sometimes they do, and then you must proceed as follows.

Deliberately under-shot the float so that an inch or so of the antenna rides out of the water. This is what you have to work to. The amount of tension you can exert on the line, in order to check the float and give correct bait presentation, is exactly the amount that will sink that antenna almost to the surface of the water. It's not much, but in the hands of an expert, it can just about be enough. It's all a matter of compromise. Leave too much antenna out of the water and you'll fail to beat the wind; also you'll have poor bite registration. Don't leave enough antenna showing and you'll have no control over the float at all.

My Swingers have buoyant Sarkanda reed antennas, and this helps you to control the float. But once you understand the basics of Swinger fishing it's very much up to you to get out there and polish up the technique. The rewards are considerable. Swingers can be used on most rivers of reasonable flow in downstream winds, and are especially useful for catching roach in these conditions. Shotting follows the basic principles concerning depth and flow that we have covered earlier. All you have to do, to get the best out of this extremely useful float, is to make sure that you're the boss.

The Arrow Float

This float came about as a result of one of my 'messing about' experiments. I'm always on the lookout for something new, and I don't mind how I discover it. Sometimes I break bits off floats to see how they work, and all sorts of silly-sounding things like that. One day I was fishing a Pacemaker, and I decided to take it off and attach it upside down, just to see what happened. Without being perfect, the result was most

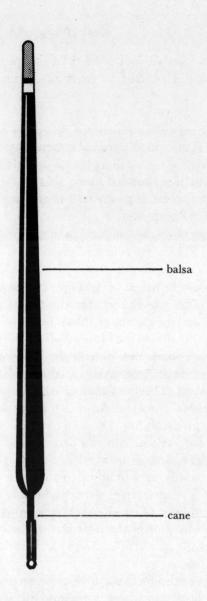

balsa

cane

Figure 14 Arrow

encouraging, so afterwards I used the principle to design the Arrow. It's not exactly an inverted Pacemaker, but almost.

Specifications: Arrows are constructed mostly of balsa. The base of the float is the widest part and it then tapers smoothly upwards towards the tip. A short length of cane is inserted into the base which is rounded down sharply to provide a streamlined taper which is pretty well the equivalent of the top shoulder of a Pacemaker.

I have a range of six, the biggest taking 5 AAA and the smallest 3 BB.

Use: Arrows should be fished bottom only in much the same way as Swingers. They work best at medium depths between five and ten feet, and they are more robust than Swingers. The larger floats will do almost the same job as the larger Balsas when downstream winds would make the Balsas difficult to control. And the small Arrows are capable of dealing with fast, shallow swims. The buoyancy of Arrows means that they ride the flow well, and it also means that the shot need to be well down to give stability. This can be further improved by putting the biggest shot directly beneath the float.

Like the Swinger, Arrows are ideal for defeating the effects of downstream winds, and in addition they can cope with rougher water. The principle of undershotting described previously should be applied when fishing Arrows. Not only does it help you to control the float but in the case of the bigger Arrows it allows you to use large baits in adverse wind and water conditions.

Altogether they are a most useful float for getting the right presentation in situations where Balsas and Swingers are not quite the answer.

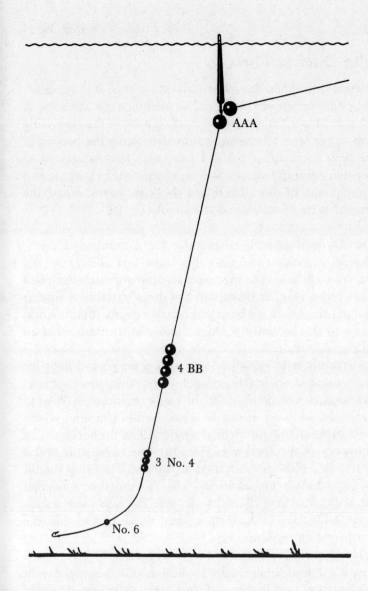

Figure 15 Typical shotting for an Arrow float

The Ducker Float

Specifications: There is a classic simplicity about the appear-ance and design of Duckers. The stem is cane, tapering in diameter from 3½ mm at the top to 2 mm, in the case of my own range, and the body, mounted towards the bottom of the float, is made of balsa. I like balsa for Duckers to be low-density stuff so that it will be as buoyant as possible and carry plenty of shot. There are six floats in my range, the biggest taking 5 AAA and the smallest 2 BB.

Use: Duckers have been popular for a number of years, largely because at one time they were just about the only answer to fishing running water in downstream winds. But more recently other floats, most of them based on a similar design principle, have been produced to cope with this situa-tion and this has left the Ducker more in the position of an all-purpose float.

Certainly it is versatile. It is still a very good float for performing its original function, one that Billy Lane, for one, has used to very good effect in bad conditions on flowing water. In addition, it can be a good stillwater float where wind makes it difficult to hold a bait still on the bottom. The buoyancy of the Ducker enables the line to be sunk and a shot to be left on the bottom as an anchor. That shot should be regarded as an additional shot to the float's normal capacity; whereas it would sink other floats in these condi-tions, a Ducker will hold up against the drag and still give sensitive bite registration.

However, now that we have Wagglers, Swingers and Arrows, I find, along with a number of other top match anglers, that the Ducker performs best a quite specific func-tion in float fishing, one that is rather specialised and has come to be known as reverse trotting.

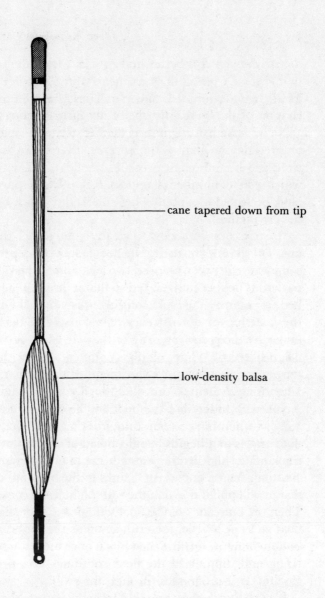

cane tapered down from tip

low-density balsa

Figure 16   Ducker

Reverse Trotting: I'd better make it clear from the beginning that reverse trotting does *not* mean trotting *against* the flow. That crazy technique is one I shall describe later in the next chapter of the book. It's one of my little eccentricities!

No, reverse trotting means deliberately allowing the float to precede the bait – the reverse, that is, of traditional trotting where the bait precedes the float. It is a technique which a small number of anglers, Robin Harris particularly, have perfected to a point where on its day it can be a really deadly method.

It works best in a slow to steady flow, rather than a fast one. This is how you do it. The float is set over-depth, usually somewhere between one and two feet, and the last shot of the pattern is deliberately placed so that it drags along the river bed. If you cast the tackle out like this you will find that as the float moves downstream it is constantly being pulled under by the recurring drag of that last shot. So you don't fish it like this. What you do is counter-balance the drag of the anchor shot by under-shotting the float further up by an amount equivalent to that shot. So, if your last shot is a No. 4, you will under-shot the float by the weight of a No. 4.

Now, when you cast out, things begin to take shape. As the float settles and begins to ride ahead of the bait, it will ride fractionally high in the water because of the slight under-shotting. As the anchor shot sinks to the bottom behind the float it will pull it down in the water to normal cocking level. Then the buoyancy of the float will lift the shot slightly, the float will rise a little, then dip again as the shot catches the bottom again. The float then lifts it once more and the slight rising and dipping of the float continues in a predictable rhythm as it progresses through the swim.

If a fish lifts the bait and shot from the bottom the float will rise higher than usual and you have a lift bite. If the fish simply takes the bait and holds it the float will submerge *at*

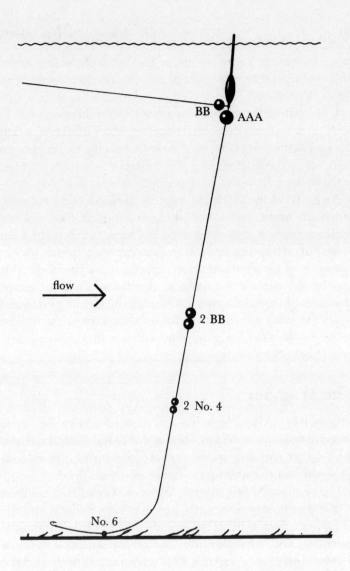

Figure 17   Ducker float shotted for reverse trotting
Note that the No. 6 dragging bottom is the exact
weight to which the float should be under-shotted

once. Either way you have bite registration of the first order and you should now be able to see why reverse trotting can be so deadly.

If the fish will take the bait presented in this way, you're on to a real winner. The intriguing aspect of this style is that the skill comes in setting up the tackle exactly, rather than in controlling the float while it is working. You can see why the word reverse is so apt in describing this style.

Now, Duckers are ideal for this method. The balance, buoyancy and combination of materials mean that you can perform the act of counter-shot balancing so that the float fishes the method to perfection. The tapered tip helps a lot. On some of the Fenland waters, particularly the Nene, this can be *the* method for slowing down your bait to tempt shy-biting bream and roach. Other floats can be persuaded to do the same job; but the Ducker seems made for it. The balsa provides the buoyancy and the cane tip the sensitivity. It's a great combination.

The Waggler

Specifications: My Wagglers are best described as slim antenna floats. The bodies are made of balsa, cylindrical and thin, rather like a cigarette. A short cane insert is fitted into the base and the antenna is Sarkanda reed.

I have a range of six, from 5 AAA down to 3 BB. Each float is exactly the same in length, just over eight inches, and the variation comes in the relationship between the body and the antenna. The 3 BB float has the largest antenna and the shortest body; the 5 AAA float has the largest body and the shortest antenna.

Use: Wagglers have several uses. For example, you are likely to see them being fished in fastish water such as the Trent, or

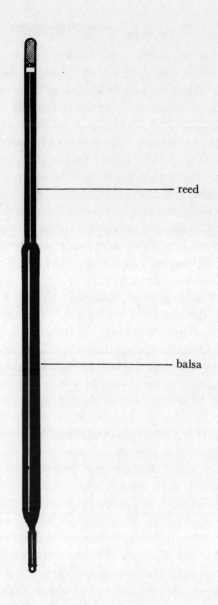

Figure 18   Waggler

on slow moving waters like the Witham, or even on still waters. And where they are used on flowing water they can be fished either like Swingers or Duckers, that is with fairly traditional bait presentation or reverse trotting.

When Waggler fishing first became fashionable the floats were often simply stillwater antennas used in running waters to beat downstream winds. Either that or they were used to fish a fair way out in strong flow. Then it was mostly a question of letting the float go at its own speed. If the float was fished over-depth it was reverse trotting, and despite the unconventional method of presenting the bait, anglers found there were days when they could catch fish. At this stage I don't think the Waggler was any special kind of float – just an antenna fished in running water.

As any method becomes popular it also becomes more specialised in the hands of the experts. And this is what happened to this kind of fishing. Skilful anglers found that with the right kind of antenna they could also hold the float back to give more traditional bait presentation. And gradually the Waggler came into being as a float in its own right.

The modern Waggler is not a robust float for rough conditions. It is a streamlined, buoyant float suitable for fishing delicate baits. It is a short- and medium-range float which, within its limitations, is multi-purpose. Usually it is associated with roach fishing, and it should not be used where the water is very deep.

For reverse trotting it should be shotted in the same way as described for the Ducker. For trotting with a sunken line at the speed of the flow it should be shotted in the same way as a Swinger, depending on depth. The same shotting is used for holding back as with the Swinger, and the float should be fished over-depth. And in still water where there is surface skim and an under-tow it can be fished as a normal still-water antenna.

What a Waggler will *not* do is anything dramatic, such as a very big cast, but it will do a number of other things well. Its versatility can be judged from the fact that often anglers will buy Wagglers and then use them to good effect in quite different conditions.

I have won matches with Wagglers on waters as different as the Trent, the Welland, the Warwickshire Avon and the Witham. It is a delicate way of fishing bottom-only, using light line and small hooks. When you become really experienced you will be able to increase your control over the float by varying the amount of line you have sunk between rod-tip and float. If you are not an expert you can at least give the Waggler a try if you are not sure which float to use. Frequently you will find it will stand you in good stead fishing a variety of styles.

Summary

Those, then, are my floats for flowing waters. They mean I am equipped to deal with different speeds of flow, different depths, near, medium or long-range casting, and various wind conditions.

From the point of view of bait presentation you may want your bait to fish anywhere from well ahead of the float to well behind it, anything between the classic stick float presentation to the reverse trotting of the Ducker. The different floats I have described will enable you to achieve what presentation you require *in all sorts of conditions*. I must add that they will also enable you to make a thorough mess of everything if you mix them up and choose the wrong float for the wrong job.

I know them so well now I don't even have to think; but if you're not so familiar with them it will pay you to read this section again until you have absorbed it fully.

Part Two : Floats for Still and Slow-Moving Waters

Pretty well all floats in this section follow the same basic principles of design, simply because they are made to cope with the particular problems posed by fishing stillwaters. Before we look at the floats I want to consider some of the basics.

Wind and surface skim

These factors are as big a problem to the stillwater float anglers as flow and boil are to the man fishing a running water. Many stillwaters and slow-moving rivers are wide and easily affected by wind. Ripples and small waves are not so difficult to overcome as surface skim. All too often the water appears calm but when you begin to fish you find the top area of water is skimming across the surface making float control difficult. The Fenland rivers are devils for surface skim, particularly the Nene.

The only way to overcome this problem is to have as small an amount of float as possible on the surface and have the line sunk and fastened quite deep under the surface to a stable float base. This is where the antenna float comes in. Unlike the conventional trotting float, which has its buoyancy near the top, the antenna float has its buoyancy well down. The idea is that only the slim antenna has to resist surface skim and wind, the bulk of the float remains stable several inches below, and the line is sunk to this depth by being attached to the base ring only.

Therefore all antenna floats used in these conditions should be fished bottom only with a sunken line. The Zoomer is an exception to this rule, but it can only be fished in perfect conditions. Beating surface skim on large lakes and some wide rivers performs two important functions: it prevents your tackle being unnaturally dragged along by the skim, and it also allows you to take advantage of the under-tow. This is very important.

Under-tow

If you are fishing a large stillwater and there is a strong surface skim from left to right, this means that the top inch or so of water is constantly being pushed to the right. How is it then that the still water stays in the same place? Why doesn't the water pile up on the shore to the right, and empty on the left? Well, of course common sense tells you it can't. The level remains constant. But the *reason* why it does is vitally important to the float angler. All that happens is that the top layer of water moving right is counterbalanced by the lower layers of water moving left. This is under-tow, and it increases as the surface skim increases.

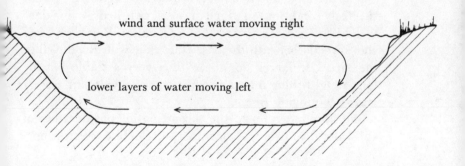

Figure 19   Under-tow

In such conditions your antenna float, correctly fished, will not only stand still against the skim. It will react lower in the water, where the bulk of the float is resting, to the movement of the lower layers of water, and it will actually move gradually *against the skim*.

Now think of your bait presentation. Your bait will, almost certainly, be low in the water, and if it was dragging in the opposite direction, as it would be if your float was captured by the skim, it would appear most unnatural. Even if your float was still, the bait would look wrong if it was motionless in under-tow. But when your float moves *with* the under-tow, so does your bait, along with other particles of food in suspension in the water. You have natural bait presentation.

The same principle applies on a slow-moving river where the skim is going in the other direction to the flow. It is only when your antenna float and sunken line beat the skim that your bait will move against it and with the flow. This situation arises frequently on waters like the Witham, the Welland and the Nene.

The design of antenna floats is therefore logical to combat the likely conditions in which they will be fished. An incidental advantage of the floats is that, cast bottom only with some shot directly beneath the base ring, they will travel well in the air. The larger floats are thus very suitable for the long-range fishing that can be necessary on wide, still waters and slow-moving rivers.

We now move on to the second basic consideration of stillwater float fishing – the importance of bite registration.

Bite registration

The floats we dealt with in the last section, the running-water floats, all had one thing in common: their first job was to present the bait correctly to the fish. That was more than half the battle, because in running water the fish have to decide quickly whether to accept the bait or not. If they dally about too long the bait will have moved on. Once they decide to bite they tend to take fairly boldly and the effects of flow and turbulence disguise to some extent the drag involved in moving the shots and float. Frequently the current will accentuate the bite, as in reverse trotting. Flowing-water fish are used to snatching food as it passes them in the water.

The situation is almost reversed in still and slow-moving waters. Except in bad weather or at extreme range, the bait presentation isn't normally too difficult; the art lies in combining it with delicate bite registration. The reason is simple. With a still or slowly moving bait a fish has plenty of time to decide whether to take it or not. And even if he takes it, he need be in no hurry and is likely to reject it if the terminal tackle is too crude or badly balanced.

Top-quality bait is therefore essential. So are fine lines and, in my opinion, small hooks. This combination helps to persuade the fish to accept the bait. But it is the sensitivity of the float and terminal tackle which allows the fish to move off with the bait and register a good bite without feeling resistance.

Don't get me wrong – sensitive bite registration is important in all float fishing. The point is that it is of crucial importance on stillwaters where the fish have so much more time to inspect the bait and feel resistance.

Therefore, in this section you will find that one of the basic considerations for most of the floats is how sensitively they can be fished. So I shall begin at the very beginning with the most sensitive of all my floats for still water.

The Special Balsa Float

Specifications: Special Balsas are not unlike the smaller floats in the normal balsa range, though they are more stream-lined. There are, however, two important differences. Special Balsas are painted black except for the very tip, which is white by contrast. And into the white balsa tip is inserted a stiff nylon bristle which is bright red.

The extreme sensitivity of these floats means that they cannot be fished at long, or even medium range, so they do not need to carry a lot of shot. My range of six goes from 4 BB down to 3 No. 4.

Use — The Pole float: The last two or three years have seen a tremendous surge of interest in this country in pole fishing. It's mostly among the match anglers that this has happened, and the influence from the Continent, particularly France, is obvious. Fished to CIPS rules, the World Championships have traditionally been dominated by Continental pole ang-lers, only England threatening that domination to any seri-ous extent. Just as European match anglers have begun to take an interest in English-style fishing, so have the English anglers started to appreciate the advantages of pole fishing, in some circumstances.

Pole fishing with a fixed line has the supreme virtue of enabling the angler to present a bait with micro-precision. The poles, some of them up to 30 feet long, stiff-actioned yet light, are used without reels. The fine fixed line on a modern pole is attached at the tip to a length of special elastic, about 14 inches long. This elastic acts as a shock absorber and enables quite powerful fish to be handled confidently on very light tackle.

The use of elastic has removed the conviction among many anglers that pole fishing is fishing for tiddlers. English

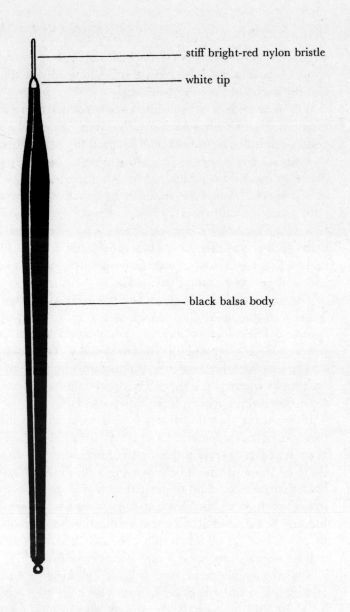

stiff bright-red nylon bristle

white tip

black balsa body

Figure 20   Special Balsa

anglers are now taking good roach and bream on a variety of
waters by using the pole. We are still a long way behind the
Continentals, but we are learning.

Pole fishing is a very limited style compared with the
range of English float-fishing techniques. But in the right
conditions it can be unbeatable. I regard the pole as being at
its best when it comes to presenting a small bait very accurately in conditions which are less than perfect.

My Special Balsas are made to be fished in conjunction
with a pole on stillwaters. Flow makes the floats less effective. If the fish are feeding well, there is no need to use these
floats. They're at their best when the fish are finicky. Then I
reckon I can get twenty times as many bites during a match
as I will get on normal float tackle.

The floats should, of course, be attached top and bottom.
There are then two vital things to get right – depth and
shotting. These factors play a very important part in Continental pole fishing, and it is easy to see why. Your long pole
and fine tackle give you every opportunity to present your
bait *exactly* where you want it. The depth and shotting are the
two other things which make this possible.

If you think that up to now I've been making a bit of a
meal out of the importance of depth, you should just see a top
French angler assessing the depth of his swim. He couldn't
try to be more precise if he was using a slide rule. What you
have to do is to attempt to present your bait *just* off bottom –
half an inch only. The idea is to place your bait where it will
literally be suspended in front of a fish's nose as it roams over
the river bed. Time taken to get the depth absolutely right
will be repaid later with a high number of bites.

Shotting comes next, and it is, if anything, even more
critical when using Special Balsas. There are two things to
get right – the amount of shot and its distribution. First, the
amount. What you need is enough shot to cock the float so

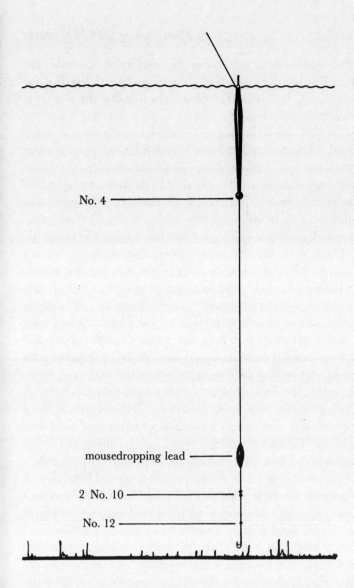

No. 4

mousedropping lead

2 No. 10

No. 12

Figure 21 Typical shotting for a Special Balsa float

that the white tip is *just* under the surface with the nylon
bristle sticking out as a sighter. The nylon helps you to locate
the white tip, but it is this tip you watch for the slightest
indication of a bite.

To get this exact cocking you'll have to use micro-shot for
the final adjustments, and you'll also have to allow for the
weight of the bait. Usually bait will be bloodworms, hemp or
casters, and although these are tiny baits and very light, the
sensitivity of Special Balsas is such that even these minute
weights have to be allowed for.

The distribution of this precise shot-load is also important. The aim is for the tackle to be fishing in its correct
position as soon as possible after it has entered the water.
After taking so much trouble to get your bait in exactly the
right place, you're not going to be worrying about bites on
the drop. In any case, using a pole you will be dropping your
terminal tackle straight into the water directly above the
place you want it to fish. You'll not be laying it across the
water as you would casting with a rod and reel.

Therefore the bulk of your shot wants to be well down. A
smallish shot directly under the float will steady it and keep
the depth accurate, but after this you want most of your shot
well below half-way, in fact closer to the hook than you
would expect if you were fishing a more conventional style.

It is normal when pole fishing to use a special kind of shot
to represent the bulk shot down below. This is known as a
Mousedropping lead. Not a very delicate name, you might
think, but it describes its elongated shape very well.

Mousedropping leads are French in origin and are
regarded on the Continent as essential to successful pole
fishing. The lead provides a compact shot load, steadies the
bait well and is very soft so that it doesn't damage the
delicate line. In fact you can use Mousedroppings over and
over again. Also their shape prevents false bites when you

are using hemp as bait. Our own traditional round shots are very like hemp in shape and can be a nuisance when fished close to a hemp-baited hook.

So, your Mousedropping weight, only inches from the hook, carries the bulk of the float's shot-capacity. You then use micro-shot between the Mousedropping and the hook to achieve exact cocking of the float and presentation of the bait. The last micro-shot can be very close to the hook, about a couple of inches away.

This may all sound a great nuisance, but believe me it can be worth it. Once you have everything set up right you've got one of the most sensitive set-ups in ;oat fishing. Through the length and stiffness of your pole you can maintain perfect contact with the float and hold it perfectly in position. Down below, the terminal tackle is so organised that the slightest bite will register instantly. In reasonable conditions you will find you can catch the shyest fish on a variety of English waters – ponds, lakes, canals, slacks in flowing rivers and on the near shelves of most of the Fenland waters.

My faith in my Special Balsas was sufficiently great for me to use one a few months ago in the 1976 World Individual Championships. I'm not generally regarded as a pole angler, but I can handle the job when necessary. Using a pole and one of my Special Balsas I finished second in these World Championships, beaten by only 3 small fish out of 190. Considering almost all the opposition were the world's best pole anglers I think it says quite a lot for my Special Balsas. Iᴌ must surely be the best recommendation I can give.

The Marks Matchsticks

Specifications: England's Glory, red-tipped, blue-tipped or black-tipped (just strike the others!).

Use: I suppose I've got to regard my matchstick fishing as a
joke. Everyone else seems to. It all started when I wrote an
article in *Angling Times* describing how I catch bleak using a
matchstick for a float. People fell about laughing! I tried to
make the same point in some detail in my book on match
fishing, but I think a lot of people think I'm having them on.

It's not true. I fish matchsticks with a double rubber when
I'm bleaking, but I don't really use them for bite registration. For that I spring the line between matchstick and hook
between my forefinger and thumb nail so that it hangs in
curly coils. These are half-submerged and half-surfaced and
it is their straightening from the pull of a fish that gives me
the bite registration.

But I can also use matchsticks as genuine floats, fished top
and bottom or peg-leg and cocked with micro-dust. And not
just to catch bleak. Fished several feet deep this rig can take
good roach and skimmers, fast. Only recently, on a demonstration, I took so many good fish in such a short time from
the margins of the Witham, using my much-laughed-at
matchstick, that John Goodwin just couldn't believe his
eyes. So I did it again for him, just in case he thought he'd
been dreaming.

If you're one of those who think my matchstick exploits
are just a bit of light-hearted publicity, then just ask him. He
knows different. He didn't laugh once! I think his eyeballs
were hurting him too much!

The Special Balsas and the Marksticks are really a separate
category of the stillwater floats. They're for extreme sensitivity at fairly close range in fair conditions. As such they're
what you could call one-off floats. The more normal range of
stillwater floats takes over where these two leave off.

The Marksman Float

This is quite a suitable float to start the full range. It can fish a similar, though not identical, style to the Special Balsa when that float is beaten by some degree of flow.

Specifications: Marksman floats are all balsa, and the main point of their design is their very slim and streamlined shape. They need to cock quickly, and the quality of balsa used must be of the correct density – not too hard and not too soft. I have a range of six floats: the two biggest take roughly 4 BB, the middle two 3 BB and the two smallest 2 BB.

Use: It helps to think of a Marksman as a float which performs much the same function as a stick float, but on still or slow-moving water.

Like the stick, a Marksman should be attached top and bottom. It is for relatively shallow water, not too far out, and it cannot be fished if conditions are rough. The float should be cast in the same way as the stick, that is underarm, so that it drops lightly across the surface and is fishing vertically from the moment it lands. Shotted like a stick float, the Marksman will give good bites on the drop. The quick cocking action is accentuated by putting a reasonably large shot directly beneath the float.

The limitations of this float are almost the same as those of its running-water equivalent, the stick. But, within its limitations, the Marksman is more versatile. It makes a very good pole float, and can cope with some flow. Since I designed this float two years ago it has proved very popular. Because it is fished top and bottom it is one of the exceptions in the range of stillwater floats. But it is a float I find most useful, not least because of the way it will sink a bait quickly to defeat bleak shoals.

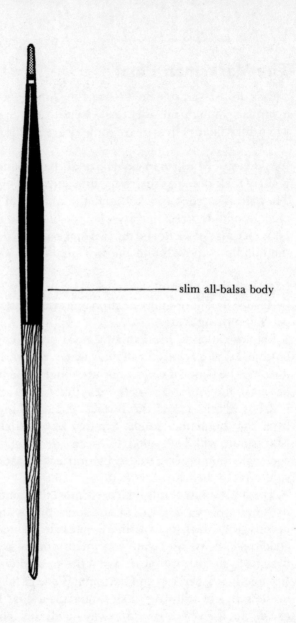

slim all-balsa body

Figure 22 Marksman

It comes into its own when the fishing is comfortable – not too deep, not too far out, not much flow, very little wind.

The Dart Float

Specifications: Darts are slim antenna floats that look rather like Wagglers in that they have long, cylindrical bodies made of balsa. But there the similarity ends, for Darts have fine, sensitive tips made of 2 mm cane. And the bottom of the float contains a brass loading. Therefore, by definition, they do not take heavy shot loads, are not suitable for rough conditions and should be fished with very fine lines and tiny hooks.

My set of Darts comprises nine floats ranging from 5 BB to 3 No. 6.

Use: I call Darts team floats, or scratching floats, because on the waters I fish they are last-resort floats, not match winners. It's only on the canals, where Darts can produce fish on the drop from the extreme far bank, that they can be reckoned as dangerous.

The Dart style involves putting most of what little shot the float will take on each side of the base ring; tiny shot are then placed well down and the float presents the bait in a slow fall. Usually the float is set over-depth so that the bait eventually rests lightly on the bottom. The float should cock so that only the minimum amount of tip is left above the surface.

There are days when only this kind of presentation will tempt fish to bite. These are the days when the fish seem off-colour, indifferent; hot days with surface glare, days after very cold nights, days when the water looks dead or lacks colour. Then you will be fishing for anything you can get; you will scale down your tackle, use your smallest baits; you will put on a Dart.

The prospect of Dart fishing, therefore, doesn't exactly get

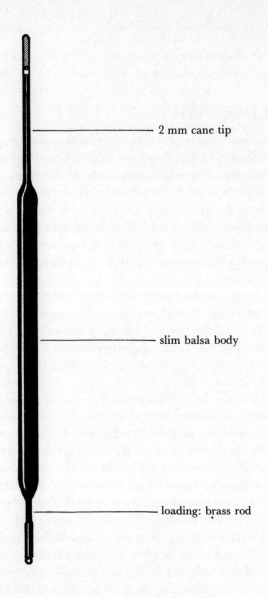

2 mm cane tip

slim balsa body

loading: brass rod

Figure 23 Dart

me quivering with excitement. It won't be a day of big weights. I'll have no chance of getting into the frame and I'll either be hoping to win a bad section or trying to get a few fish for a team weight. You see, the float is too limited to be a winner. It's too slow, it can't cope with surface skim because it can't take the shot down below and because the antenna is too sensitive; in fact, it's geared to a static style of fishing that you only resort to when you can't think of anything else. Furthermore, a Dart can't be used effectively at long range or in deep water.

Why then, you may ask, do I trot around the country with a range of nine Darts? The answer is simply that there are times when nothing but a Dart will produce a few fish. The float itself does its job well, it's a must for every match angler and can play a vital part in modern National Championships under the points system.

It's not that I don't like the float – it's just that I don't look forward to the times when I'm forced to use it!

There are sixteen different kinds of floats in my stillwater range. That is rather a lot for you to remember easily by the time I've dealt with them all. So what I'll do is try to group them under three main headings, to make things easier.

Now, the four floats I've just described – the Special Balsa, the matchstick, the Marksman and the Dart – you can regard as being of the most limited use. They all need fair wind and water conditions and they don't cope well with deep water. Therefore they are for short-range fishing when things are fairly comfortable. They are also of special value when fish are hard to come by.

Next, we come to a group of six different floats which *between them* will allow you to increase the scope of your stillwater fishing – that is, cope with stronger winds and skim, more depth and longer range. I am *not* saying that any one of these floats will do all these things, and none of them belongs to the final group which are the long-range, deep-water floats.

So, this next group will take you a little further – in several senses of the word. They are all antenna floats and are invariably fished bottom only. In the order in which I shall deal with them they are: 2 mm (short, canal) antennas, 2 mm loaded canal antennas, 2 mm (long, canal) antennas, 2 mm Slimlines, Javelins, and tipped swingers.

2 mm (Short, Canal) Antennas

Specifications: These are very short antenna floats with a quite stubby balsa body fitted to the base of a length of 2 mm cane. The tip of the antenna is marked with a broad red band, moving down through a narrow black band to a broad white one. This deep banding of the tip is to make clear to the angler the bites on the drop and the lift bites which are a feature of this float. The slim cane antenna will lift or sink at least half an inch simply by the weight of one small shot.

I have three of these floats taking 5, 4 and 3 BB.

Use: These are short floats, so they can't work properly in deep water. Six feet is about the maximum. Neither will they perform in wind and waves, because of the extreme sensitivity of the 2 mm antenna. They will, however, cope with a certain amount of surface skim, and they will cast a fair way for their size.

They are at their best at close to medium range on a big river, or fished right across on a small one. They will resist a slow pull on the water but are defeated by flow. This is why they are extremely useful on canals, where their sensitivity is invaluable in registering bites from small or shy-biting fish.

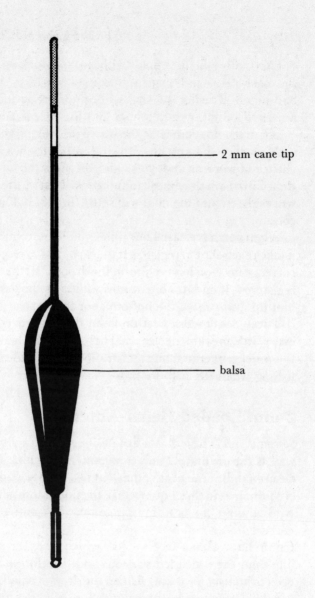

2 mm cane tip

balsa

Figure 24   2 mm (short, canal) antenna

I normally fish these floats with two shot locking the line to the base ring, and then a cluster of working shot below half-depth. The bottom shot will be just off bottom, but the float will be set over-depth so that the bait is laid on.

When the float lands on the water the locking shot cocks it with most of the antenna sticking out of the water. As the cluster of working shot sinks and registers the antenna will drop in the water almost to full cock. Lastly, the final shot will register, and the float will settle the last half inch to full cock.

When you have cast a few times you'll know just how long it takes each shot to register. If the float fails to respond at the correct time, you have a bite on the drop. If all the shots have registered, then bites often show as lifts as the fish picks the bait up and causes the bottom shot to rise.

These floats work best on calm days when you can see every little movement clearly. They give a particularly sensitive and exaggerated bite registration and one ideal for roach fishing when the fish are biting shyly.

2 mm Loaded Canal Antennas

Specifications: These floats are designed in exactly the same way as the ordinary 2 mm canal antennas which I have just described. But the base of the float has a brass loading which is equivalent to three-quarters of the float's total shot capacity. The three floats in my range take 3, 2 and 1 BB.

Use: What we have here is a float which takes less shot on the line than the unloaded version, and therefore it should be used primarily for taking fish on the drop in small rivers and canals. There is less opportunity for defeating any skim or pull because the float itself carries most of the shot-loading. But in the right conditions you have an ideal float for getting

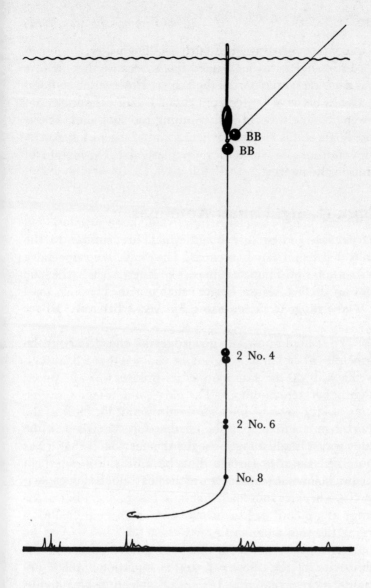

Figure 25   Typical shotting for a 2 mm antenna

a quick bite registration in fairly shallow water.

Many anglers favour loaded floats because they involve less shotting on the part of the angler. However, such floats must always be of limited application because the angler has fewer possible ways of redistributing the shot-load. Therefore floats of this kind in particular must be fished in exactly the conditions for which they were designed. The margin for abuse is negligible.

2mm (Long, Canal) Antennas

Specifications: These are floats which are similar to the unloaded 2 mm canal antennas. They have the same balsa bodies and slim 2 mm antennas. The difference is in the size; they are, in fact, bigger, longer versions of the previous float. I have a range of three, taking 3 AAA, 4 BB and 3 BB.

Use: You should now be knowledgeable enough about the principles of design to work out for yourself that a float such as this will do the same job as its predecessor but under slightly trickier conditions. The long 2mm antenna has the same ability to show bites on the drop and lift bites as the short 2 mm antenna. It should therefore be fished in the same way. Its advantage over the shorter float is that it has more resistance to surface drag because the line is held further below the surface. It will also cast further because it carries a heavier shot load. There is, however, a limit to the range at which it can be fished because of the difficulty in seeing the slim antenna tip.

Even so, it is not a big float. It simply passes on the sensitivity of the shorter floats to situations which are slightly more demanding. It's not suitable for fishing depths over six feet, and is at its best on the bigger canals, small drains and stillwaters.

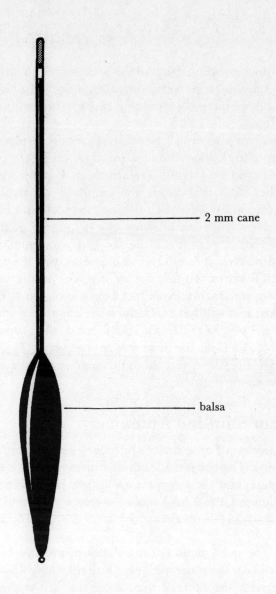

2 mm cane

balsa

Figure 26   2 mm (long, canal) antenna

The quick cocking action of the previous two floats is maintained in this larger version by the angler continuing to put about three-quarters of the shot capacity immediately under the float.

You can also expect to achieve the best results with fine line and tiny hooks. Although this is the biggest float we have looked at so far, it is still a relatively close-range, reasonable weather float that keeps the emphasis on sensitive bite registration, mostly when fishing for roach and bream.

Perhaps you're wondering why it can't be used in fairly deep water, more than the six feet maximum I recommended. Well, it can, but it would be wasting the float's best design features. To fish deeper involves putting more shot well down to maintain contact from hook to float. When you do this, you will have to reduce the amount of shot that is immediately beneath the float. And then your quick-cocking, bites on the drop feature has gone.

Logically, then, you should change to the next float, the 2 mm slimline antenna.

2 mm Slimline Antennas

Specifications: These floats are bigger versions of the 2 mm antenna. The body, made of soft, buoyant balsa, is more oval in shape, and the antennas are longer in the bigger floats. The longest, the 4 AAA model, is nine inches, and the other four floats in this range take 3 AAA, 2 AAA, 3 BB and 2 BB.

Use: The introduction of the slimline antennas means that you can get the same bite registration and sensitivity as you have with the other 2 mm antennas, but *in deeper water*. Whereas the previous floats have had a depth maximum of six feet, these Slimlines are designed to work best from six feet to twelve feet.

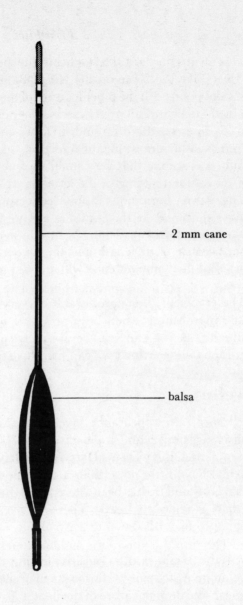

2 mm cane

balsa

Figure 27   2 mm Slimline antenna

This means they are ideal for fishing deeper inshore ledges on rivers like the Nene on the North Bank, or fairly deep lakes and ponds. All the other features of the 2 mm range are retained – delicate bait presentation, magnified bite registration for bites on the drop and lift bites. And the shotting pattern will be almost identical, except that the balance of Slimlines is so fine that very small shot near the hook will register on the banding of the antenna tip.

The same limitations apply concerning range. The heavier shot-loads of the Slimlines are not for extra casting distance but for extra depth. Naturally the float will resist skim, because of its length and the amount of shot downstairs. But the 2 mm antenna will not take a lot of wind and waves.

The emphasis, therefore, is still on very sensitive, fairly close-range fishing when bites are hard to come by. But gradually, as you can see, we are increasing the range of conditions under which we can fish this style.

Javelins

Specifications: In appearance Javelins are similar to Darts, with a long, slim, cylindrical body made of balsa, and a 2 mm cane antenna. But whereas Darts have a definite antenna the Javelins have little more than a tip. The relationship between body and tip has been altered, and the body loading at the base is relatively heavy. There are five sizes of Javelin, ranging from 3 BB down to 2 No. 4.

Use: If the Slimlines allow sensitive fishing in depth, then the Javelins give the same performance in unpleasant wind conditions. The design feature of the float is how well it casts in unfavourable winds – not heavy winds, just nasty ones. It is therefore well-named.

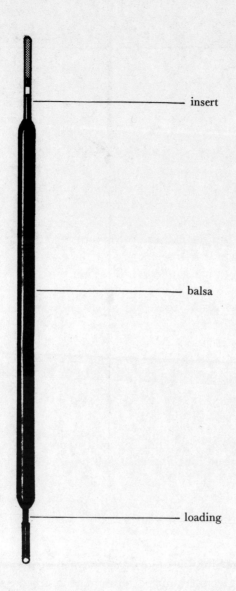

insert

balsa

loading

Figure 28 Javelin

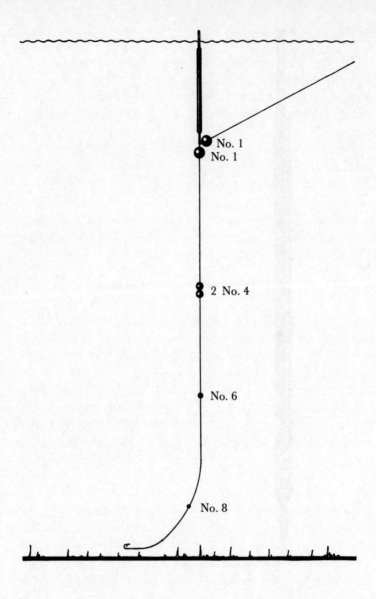

No. 1
No. 1

2 No. 4

No. 6

No. 8

Figure 29   Typical shotting for a Javelin float

The brass loading means that the float cocks instantly, and the relatively light shotting downstairs makes it an excellent float for fishing on the drop. The long body gives good stability and the slim tip provides sensitivity to show lift bites.

The float is not designed to fish deep water, nor does it work properly in flow. What it does quite beautifully is to allow the same delicate bait presentation as the other floats, but in above-water conditions that would make them difficult to cast and handle properly. Altogether they are very useful floats for fishing on exposed stillwaters and slow-moving rivers where conditions are not as calm as you would like.

Tipped Swingers

Specifications: This is one of my most recent designs and it combines the advantages of the Swinger floats described in the last section and the cane-tipped antennas I have been mentioning over the last few pages.

The float has the basic features of a Swinger, with a streamlined balsa body set low on a Sarkanda reed antenna. But there is a 2 mm cane insert in the top of the Sarkanda which gives the same inch of tip as the Javelins. At one time it wasn't possible to put slim inserts into antenna floats on a commercial basis – the cost was too high. The only floats you could get with inserts, usually peacock quill, were hand-made floats. In fact I made all my insert floats myself until we found a way of producing the floats by machine at competitive prices.

I'm very pleased with this development as it has meant that we are now able to provide anglers with a range of conventional floats with inserts for added sensitivity. At the moment, in addition to tipped Swingers, we are marketing tipped Sarkanda reed antennas and tipped Zoomers.

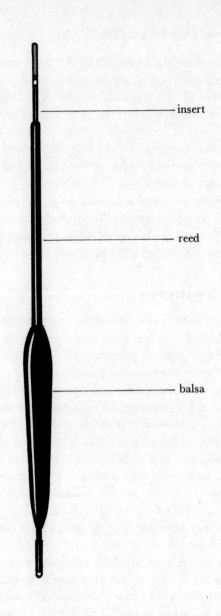

— insert

— reed

— balsa

Figure 30   Tipped Swinger

The range of three tipped Swingers have identical bodies but different lengths of antenna. The shot capacity of all three floats is approximately 3 AAA.

Use: You'll perhaps remember that the job of an ordinary Swinger is to present a bait properly in flowing water when the wind is tricky. It therefore has a buoyant Sarkanda antenna to resist drag.

The tipped Swinger employs the same design for much the same reason, but the cane insert gives sensitivity rather than buoyancy in the tip because it does not have to cope with flow. The tipped Swinger is therefore a float which should be used on still or sluggish waters. It can present a bait on the drop, or laid on, depending on how you place the shotting. By now you should know how to organise this. The limited shot capacity means that this is still a long-distance float, or one for fishing in deep water. But it gives you a choice of three different lengths for beating drift and moderate wind, yet retains great sensitivity in bite registration.

Together with the Javelin the tipped Swinger is the most versatile of the short-range, super-sensitive stillwater floats which are nevertheless able to cope with less pleasant conditions than the first group of four.

We now come to the final six of my stillwater floats, and in various degrees they represent the third and final stage – float fishing either at long or extreme range, often in deep or deepish water, and sometimes in rough winds.

Earlier in this book I warned beginners against being too ambitious with long-range floats, and I must repeat that warning here. It is quite definitely more difficult to fish a float at long range in rough conditions than it is close in, and

you ought to master the first two groups of floats before you
get carried away with the idea of thrashing big Missiles into
orbit.

You will notice that each range of floats begins with the
shortest float carrying the least shot. The range progresses so
that each float is longer and carries more shot. This is not
true of some of the floats in other ranges, e.g. the Darts and
sticks. The point about the two-fold progression of this range
is that you choose your float according to any of three
conditions: the depth of the water, the distance to be cast,
and the strength of drag, skim or wind. The more extreme
any of these conditions, the larger the float should be and the
more shot it should take.

Therefore each of the biggest floats in this last group of six
is a long-range float, but the smaller ones may be used at
medium range when conditions are good. As a general rule
you use the smallest float that will cope properly with the
particular conditions under which you are fishing.

Broadly speaking, these floats are associated with catching bream on the wide Fenland rivers, or on lakes. They have
been very carefully designed so that they will cast well; the
flight of the float in the air must be true and decisive. It
should not loop or wobble about. Given a good float, you
must shot it correctly to achieve perfect flight across the
water.

All these floats should be fished bottom only with an
overhead cast, apart from the Zoomer. They are made to
help you to get bait presentation in difficult to extreme
conditions, and therefore sensitive bite registration has to be
sacrificed to some extent. Naturally, I make sure the floats
are as sensitive as possible, bearing in mind the job they have
to do. But common sense will tell you, for example, that an
antenna float fished forty yards out in heavy surface ripple
just can't have a 2 mm tip – you couldn't see it.

Generally speaking, then, these aren't roach floats, though the smaller versions can be useful for roach in good conditions, particularly the floats with inserts. They are floats for bigger fish, usually bream, and therefore the extreme sensitivity of bite registration is not so essential. The main problem is to get your bait out to, and down to, the fish.

Shotting

Shotting is standard throughout the range of floats, provided that the depth is over six feet, and it invariably is. The float is locked onto the line with two or more large shot, and it's a good idea to use two short pieces of silicone or valve rubber between the two shots either side of the base ring. Long-casting with heavy terminal tackle, and striking at range into heavy fish, imposes a strain at this point and the rubbers act as shock absorbers. I'd advise you to use a line of at least 2½ lb breaking strain when fishing the larger floats, and 3 lb would perhaps be advisable if you're not very experienced.

The large shot at the float base should use at least half of the float's shot capacity, and in most cases you can increase this to almost two-thirds. Remember that apart from the Zoomer these floats are not loaded, they take a fair amount of shot, and most of this needs to go directly underneath the float for two important reasons – first, to enable the float to be cast properly, and second, to cock it partly as it lands so that you can spot bites on the drop.

The second group of shots, the bulk of what shot are left to complete the capacity, should *always* be positioned just below half-way down the line between float and hook. There are three reasons for this. The first is to achieve the best position for giving the float perfect flight on the cast. The second is to prevent the hook back-tangling with the float on

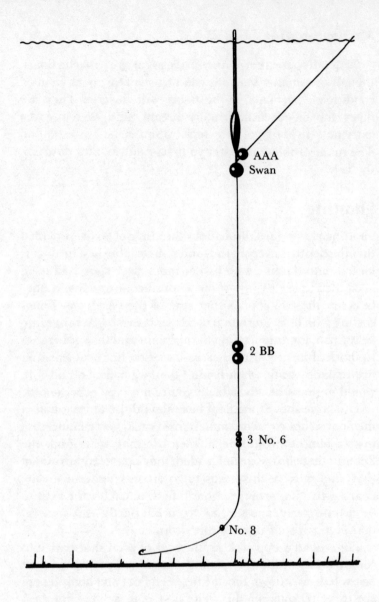

AAA
Swan

2 BB

3 No. 6

No. 8

Figure 31 Typical shotting for a reed antenna float

the cast. The third is to sink the first half of the terminal tackle quickly to bring the float to three-quarter cock. I call these shot the bulk shot, and I always use more than one shot in this position so I can slide one or more up or down if I need to change the bait presentation.

Pause a minute and consider what we have so far. We've a big antenna float heavily shotted at the base. As soon as it hits the water it begins to cock, the bulk shot sink to half depth and the float settles further in the water. Where is the baited hook at this point? Think carefully. If we have no other shot on the line, it will still be close to the surface, and in the process of sinking slowly with its own weight so that it will gradually pass the bulk shot and flutter to the bottom.

The final, small shots that you will add will therefore determine the rate at which the bait falls, and the large shot you have used so far will have no effect on the presentation. Your last groups of working shot can therefore vary the presentation from fishing on the drop to being laid on. If you want to fish on the drop, add most of the remaining shot to the bulk shot, and just place a small shot between them and the hook. If you want to fish hard on the bottom, perhaps to counter any pull in the water, put your working shot well down and if necessary bring down one of the bulk shot to join them if you are having difficulty in holding bottom. And if you want a compromise between the two, put two or more groups of small working shot between the bulk shot and the hook.

Normally you will fish these floats over-depth, on average by about 1½ feet. It helps, however you have shotted the rest of the tackle, if you can arrange to have your final shot exactly on the depth, or very fractionally off bottom. This shot needs to be big enough to register a lift bite on the particular float you are using.

Perhaps now you can see why a big float taking a lot of shot is not necessarily a crude piece of tackle. Properly balanced, the terminal tackle is still sensitive, and when a fish bites it is only affecting a small amount of the float antenna. All the rest of the float's buoyancy is permanently counteracted by the locking shot and the bulk shot. Of course, if the shotting is badly distributed and the float out of balance you will have an abomination of a thing that wouldn't catch fish under any circumstances.

Right, now you have a clear idea of how this last group of floats work, we'll look in more detail at them individually.

The Sarkanda Reed Antenna

Specifications: This is perhaps the basic float for long-range fishing. It is the modern commercial equivalent of the peacock quill antenna. The floats are unloaded with a streamlined balsa body, a short cane insert at the base, and a long antenna made of Sarkanda reed.

Peacock quill is very similar to Sarkanda reed in that it is very buoyant and fairly delicate. However, it is difficult to find a plentiful supply of top-quality quills, whereas Sarkanda can be obtained in quantity. It has the further advantage of being uniformly straight and comes in a suitable range of diameters. When it was first used as a substitute for peacock quill there were some initial problems in getting the painted finish perfect, but these have now been overcome.

I have two separate ranges of six floats each, the first going from 7 AAA to 5 BB and the second from 3 swan shot down to 2 AAA.

Use: Since these floats are the standard design for long-range stillwater fishing, they should be used in exactly the ways I have described in the introductory paragraphs to this final group of floats.

You'll find that the thickness and buoyancy of the antenna

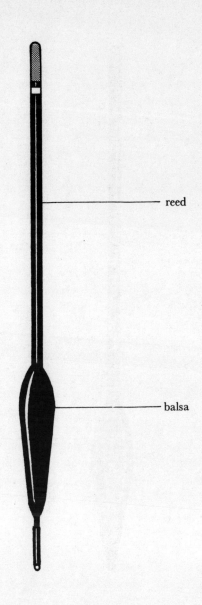

reed

balsa

Figure 32(a)   Reed antenna – Set 1

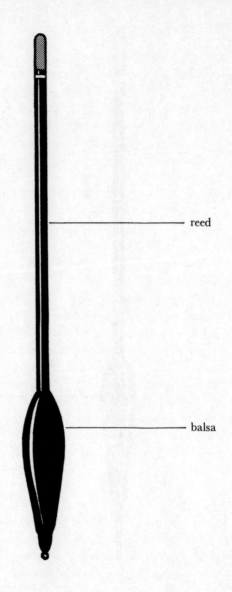

reed

balsa

Figure 32(b)   Reed antenna – Set 2

tip will mean that this float can be seen clearly at maximum range and will ride confidently through surface drift, wind and waves. Provided you distribute the shot as I advised, you shouldn't have any tangles on the cast. But if a cross wind gives you any difficulties, don't forget to cast across and *into* it, rather than the easier-sounding alternative of across and with the wind. On long casts remember to over-cast slightly, then bury the rod tip in the water, reel in sharply a few turns and sink your line. Almost all the advantages of the float's design will be wasted if you don't sink your line.

After that you should maintain close contact with your float. A slight pull on the line, or a quarter turn of the reel handle, should sink the float immediately. And at long range the strike should be a powerful sweep because you have an awful lot of line to pick up on that strike, as well as allowing for its elasticity.

The biggest floats in this range are suitable for fishing the largest stillwaters and slow-moving rivers – even the Great Ouse Relief Channel. The smaller floats allow you to fish narrower rivers in bad conditions. Just bear in mind, though, that once you have the technique to fish these floats at long range, you'll also need to be able to feed your swim just as accurately.

The Tipped Sarkanda Reed Antenna

Specifications: These floats are exactly the same in construction and design as the normal reed antennas, but with one modification: the last inch on the antenna is replaced with a 2 mm cane insert. Because of this, the length of float is different for an equivalent shot-capacity.

Use: Technically the tipped antennas are fished the same as the conventional antenna. The difference in performance is

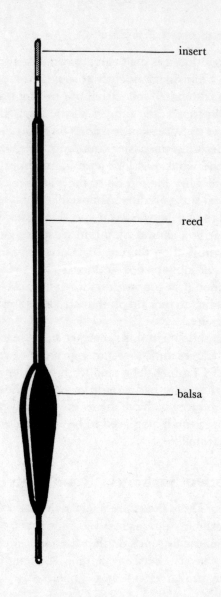

Figure 33 Tipped antenna

the increased sensitivity at the tip, providing less resistance to a biting fish. The final load of working shot needs, of course, to be adjusted more finely to set the slim cane tip.

The advantage is that on hard-fished waters the difference in resistance can just be enough to enable you to get bites that would not have registered with the untipped float. You still have all the useful features of long-casting ability and being able to fish a deeply sunken line. But at any great range you need good eyesight to spot the slim antenna.

These floats are particularly useful for fishing at distance in lakes. Of course they can't cope as well as the conventional float with rough winds or any degrees of hard pull; then you need the added diameter and buoyancy of normal reed antennas. But I find them an invaluable part of my range and I regard them as either long-range floats for ideal conditions, or medium-range floats for waters where bites are shy. The smallest floats in the range are suitable for achieving the same ends in waters which are not too wide or deep.

The Sarkanda antennas, tipped and untipped, are suitable for a wide range of conditions, the remaining floats in this last group becoming increasingly specialised. We begin with the Reverse Ducker.

Reverse Duckers

Specifications: The Ducker floats, which I described in the previous section as being ideal for reverse trotting, were, you may remember, balsa-bodied floats with a soft cane antenna tapering upwards from 2 mm to 3½ mm. The Reverse Ducker is a similar float but the antenna taper has been reversed – 3½ mm at the bottom tapering to 2 mm at the tip.

There are six floats in the range, the largest taking 2½ swan shot and the smallest 3 BB.

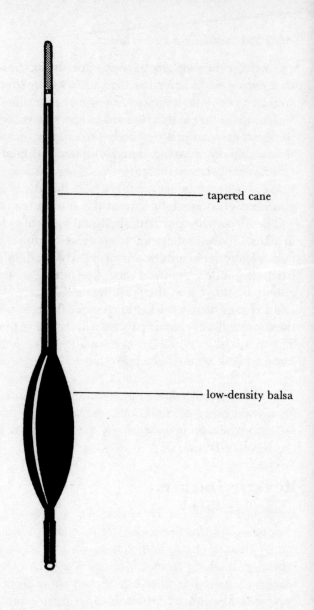

tapered cane

low-density balsa

Figure 34   Reverse Ducker

Use: Reverse Duckers are very suitable, in the largest sizes, for fishing both depth and distance where nasty winds cause casting problems and vicious surface skim. The narrowness of the tip of the antenna does not make it ideal for *rough* winds which whip up the water. It's those gusting, flat winds which make the water surface race along that this float can handle best. This is because the wider antenna base helps stability and the slim tip minimises the pull of the skim. Reverse Duckers therefore give you an advantage over conventional parallel antennas in conditions such as I've just described.

The floats cast well, ride well and are yet sensitive. Although they were designed for certain stillwater situations, their shape gives them a certain versatility so that some anglers find them equally useful on running water, fished as Wagglers. This is partly because, for an antenna float, they are relatively short.

We are now left with the two 'big boys', both loaded floats – the Missile and the Zoomer. Between them these floats provide the final coverage of all possible conditions, and I have left them until last – the Missile because it is for *extreme* range, and the Zoomer because for me it is the most specialised float of all, and the one with which my name is most associated.

The Missile

Specifications: Missiles are the heaviest floats I use. They have plump balsa bodies and antennas made of wide-diameter Sarkanda reed. The base of the float has a heavy brass loading which is carefully calculated in relation to the length of the float so that it flights perfectly during the cast.

I have two Missiles: the smaller one is 10 inches long and takes 4 AAA; the larger version is 10½ inches long and takes

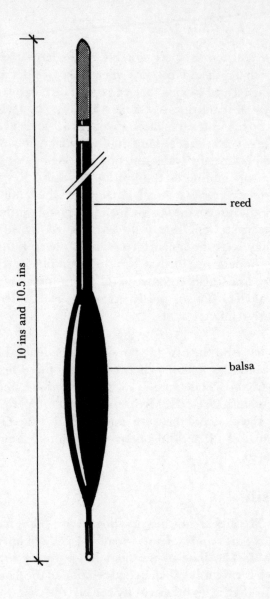

Figure 35 Missile

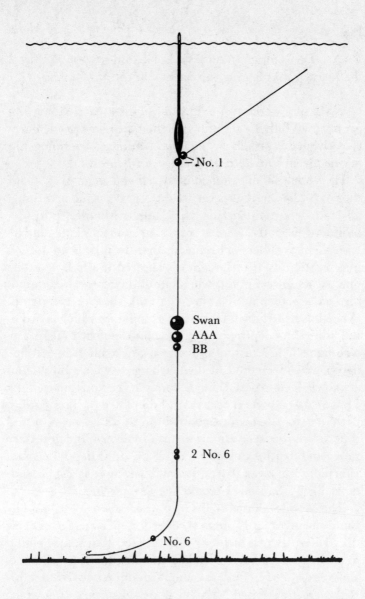

Figure 36   Typical shotting for a Missile. Note the bulk loading
at mid-water

5 AAA. Don't forget that these shot loadings are *in addition to* the heavy brass loading already built into the floats.

Use: Missiles were invented by one of the great float anglers of our time, Billy, Lane. Billy designed the floats particularly for Coventry's attack on the 1966 National Championship on the Great Ouse Relief Channel in Norfolk.

The venue should immediately tell you something about the float. The Channel is very wide, very deep and invariably affected by strong surface drag. Billy's Missiles, purpose-built for this water, were at least sixteen inches long, and he used them as sliders. This means that the float is not locked into position by two shots but is allowed to run free on the line. At its lowest point, when out of the water, it comes to rest on a shot placed above the bulk shot at mid-depth. When it is fished the float rises to a stop-knot which is tied to the line at the depth you finally want the float to fish. The technique helps casting when you are fishing at extreme depth. It is a method of float fishing at which Billy is an acknowledged expert, though I am not keen on it myself. As I have said on several occasions, I don't like the limited shot pattern associated with slider fishing, and I hardly ever find it necessary because almost always I can cast the necessary range and depth by using a fixed float. If the depth becomes ridiculous, say over 20 feet, I would perhaps use a slider, but more likely than not I would opt for legering.

The Missile comes into its own where a long cast – and by that I mean 30 yards plus – is called for, on waters over 8 feet deep where there is little or no flow. Places that come to mind at once are big lakes, the Relief Channel, the North Bank of the Nene, the Huntspill and the Witham. A deeply sunk line to a correctly shotted Missile will defeat surface drag which on these waters often causes lighter floats to be dragged *against* the natural pull of the water.

Your line needs to be of a breaking strain of at least 2½ lb, preferably 3 lb, as the strain on the tackle can be considerable. Above all you *must not snatch* on the cast – it should be smooth and easy or you will suffer from shock impact breakages. Almost all the shot should be positioned just below half depth, with a few working shot nearer the hook. If you are fishing the Missile as a fixed float you should use the smallest practical shots as lock-shots, so as not to upset the balance of the float's loading. If you fish the Missile as a slider these lock-shot can become a single stop-shot placed about a foot above the bulk shot. Where back-tangles are a problem you'll have to sacrifice some of the flexibility of the working shot by putting on relatively large shot near the hook.

Missiles can achieve such sensational range that their limit is more likely to be determined by how far you can throw your feed rather than by the limitations of the floats themselves. However, if wind conditions are favourable and the water isn't too deep, I'll go every time for the other, and final, long-range float in my series, and that's the Zoomer.

The Zoomer

There are Zoomers, and Zoomers. In the sixties Leicester anglers developed the Zoomer as a very special float for fishing the Welland. Our successes with it since have been unsurpassed. However, the Welland Zoomer is so specialised that it is only when it has been modified slightly that it can be confidently used by other anglers on a variety of waters.

Therefore I shall deal first with my commercial range of Zoomers, not quite Welland Specials, but very popular floats which have helped many anglers to catch a lot of fish.

I shall then finish this account of all my floats by telling

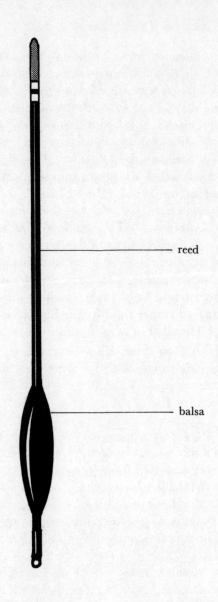

reed

balsa

Figure 37   Ordinary Zoomer

you about a float that I find particularly useful – my own, hand-made Zoomer.

Specifications: Zoomers are antenna floats with plump balsa bodies, brass loading in the base and a Sarkanda reed antenna. They are very much like the scaled-down Missiles. There are six floats in the range. The biggest, 5 AAA, is similar in size to my hand-made special, and the other five floats range down to 2 BB.

Use: The smaller Zoomers are ideal for fishing bottom only on relatively shallow and narrow stillwaters. The larger Zoomers perform best at long range in water of medium depth. They excel when there is a slight pull to the river, and if the wind is slightly behind and upstream they can be fished top and bottom. Then you can control the float's progress and present a slowly moving bait to tempt shy bream.

Fished bottom only, the large Zoomers can still be controlled to some extent because of the buoyancy of the antenna. One of the functions of the float is to show lift bites and your terminal shotting should be arranged so that this is possible. Because the Zoomer is a relatively short float for a heavy shot capacity antenna, it follows that it is not ideal for rough conditions.

Using the Zoomer in these different ways, many anglers have found that it is a very useful long-range float. Fished top and bottom, it should be cast underarm. What you are then getting at long range is some of the variety of bait presentation and sensitivity that you would normally only expect from close-range fishing.

Tipped Zoomers

These floats bear the same relationship to ordinary Zoomers

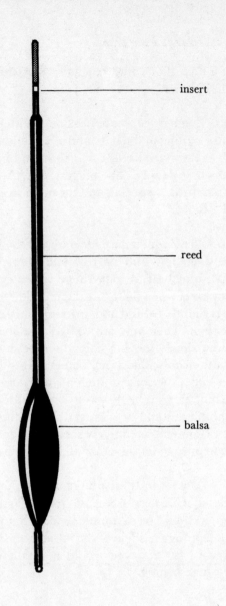

Figure 38   Tipped Zoomer

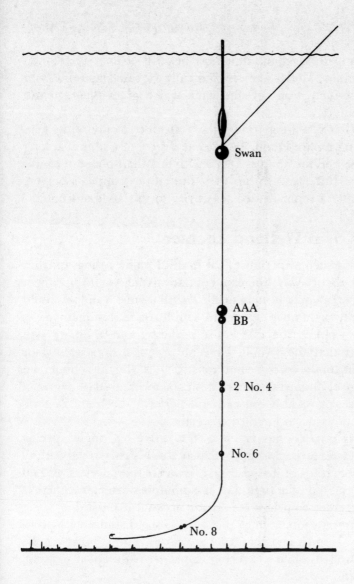

Figure 39 Typical shotting for ordinary Zoomer float

as tipped Sarkanda antennas bear to ordinary Sarkanda antennas. That is, they are basically the same floats but with a one-inch insert of slim cane which gives them greater sensitivity.

What you are getting is less resistance to shy-biting fish. What you are sacrificing is some degree of visibility at long range and the ability to cope with less-than-pleasant conditions. But, used within their limitations, tipped Zoomers provide a sophisticated sensitivity to this style of fishing.

My own Welland Zoomer

This is such a specialist float that if I made a thousand and gave them away, the chance that anyone would use them properly would be next to nil. To sell them at random would simply be lumbering anglers with floats that in many cases they wouldn't be able to use properly, and in others with floats that they would have no practical opportunity for fishing in the correct conditions. That is why my commercial range of Zoomers has been designed to stand some degree of abuse, or misuse, yet can still perform the basic Zoomer functions when handled correctly.

My own Zoomer is a one-off creation – a single, specific float with no compromise whatsoever. Fished wrongly in any respect it is not just useless, it is worse than useless. Fished correctly, on the right day, it cannot be beaten. Yet there is no secret about how it is made or what it must do.

First, its job. It must cast a very long distance with accuracy. It must register lift bites clearly. It must be able to be controlled while it is being fished. It is designed to catch bream.

After a great deal of experiment I came up with a design which in my opinion cannot be bettered. It consists of an antenna float exactly 8½ inches long with a plump balsa

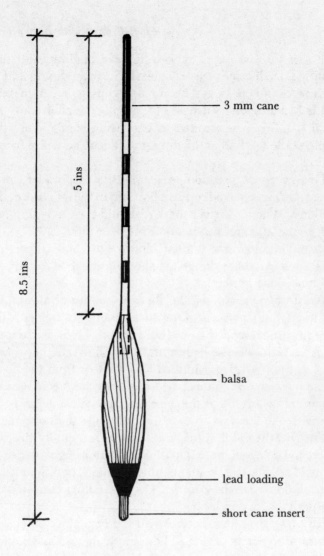

Figure 40   Ivan's special Zoomer. Note that this float *must* carry
at least a further 2 swan shot on the line and it should
be fished top and bottom

body. In the base is a hand-built lead loading, and this
loading is such that it leaves at least 2½ swan shot to add to
the line for full cocking. The antenna consists of 3 mm cane
and is 5 inches long. Instead of the tip being painted in the
usual banding it is marked in very wide bands along the
whole of the top half of the antenna. Black and white bands
are best.

This eccentric creation must now be cast underarm –
repeat, *underarm* – fixed top and bottom, to the far bank of the
Welland. When it arrives there it should cock to within one
inch of the antenna tip, it should register both bites on the
drop and lift bites, and it must allow me to control it perfectly. To achieve these things the shotting must be exact, and
the conditions perfect.

Within two variations, the shotting cannot be altered, or
the float won't perform. One swan shot goes beneath the
base ring and a second swan shot goes just below half depth.
An AAA is placed above this, and a working shot, between a
No.1 and a No.4, is positioned about a foot from the hook.
The only variation to this pattern is if the AAA is moved up
to join the swan shot at the base ring. The ideal depth is 7-8
feet with the float set so that the bait trips the bottom.

The weather and water conditions are equally precise.
There must be a slight pull to the water, and a light upstream
wind, ideally upstream and behind. If these conditions don't
prevail, don't use the Zoomer. Use something else – a Missile perhaps, or the leger.

All these strict instructions will fall into place when you
see the Zoomer in action. The underarm cast and perfect
flight mean that the float can be laid right along the far bank.
It cocks immediately and settles down to two inches of
antenna protruding as the bulk shot register. The tell-tale
shot is capable of sinking the antenna another whole inch
(remember it's made of hard 3 mm cane). If a bream takes

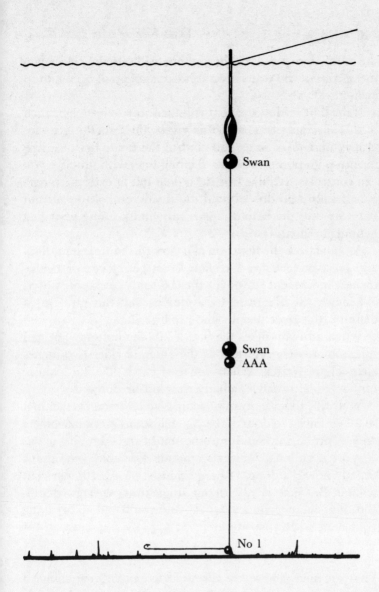

Figure 41   The correct shotting for Ivan's special Zoomer

the bait before it settles, the antenna will remain a clear two inches out of the water – an unmistakable bite on the drop even at 40 yards.

If the bait settles, the float will then sink to leave one inch of the antenna clear, and this gives you something to see clearly and work to as you control the float. Because it is fixed top and bottom with a floating line, with practice you can control it. It's like trotting a float but at extreme range. You couldn't do this without the steady pull of the current one way and the helpful upstream wind keeping your line behind the float.

As you check the float you can vary the bait presentation, and on a perfect day I reckon I can get eleven or twelve inches movement through the bottom layers of water. Whenever the bream prefer a moving bait this gives me a definite edge over people who are legering.

When a bream takes the bait it lifts the bottom shot and this immediately registers as the antenna rides two inches clear of the water. When you can catch like this you're untouchable, because nobody else will be doing it.

You will, though, from now on! I've told you everything, so all you need to do is make yourself some special Zoomers and get practising. But I must be honest and admit it's not as easy as it sounds. However, just as I've told you, that's exactly how it's done. It's a glorious style – a 101 per cent winner. But just try it with one single thing wrong – depth, shotting, balance, flow or wind – and you'll end up breaking your float with frustration.

———

That's it then. Those are all my floats, and I'm sticking to 'em. Show me any stretch of water in this country where fish can be caught, and I'll show you a float and a style that will catch them. If they'll feed, of course!

To try and show you the different kinds of floats, and how one takes over where another leaves off, I've had to organise and order them for you. But don't imagine I have all my floats laid out in sequence, with an instruction pamphlet for each. It's all there in my head somewhere is what I say. More often than not I don't seem to think why I'm doing what I'm doing. Explaining everything to you has taken years off my life, I'm sure!

You may not be able to remember all we've gone over so far (you may not want to, either!) but at least you should now have a fair idea of the basics of float fishing and that there is a float for every job if you take the trouble to work it out.

Now I'd like to explain how, once you have the knowledge, you can build still further upon it to make yourself a really successful angler.

4 The Secrets of My Success

I DON'T REALLY have any secrets if you define secrets as knowledge that you keep to yourself, deliberately. But there are a number of reasons why I may be catching fish that you can't realise just by watching me. You can see my casting and striking, the float I'm using and the depth, even the shotting. But there are many other little things that added together are very important, and these things I want to explain in this chapter. They're not so much secrets as things you may not realise unless they are pointed out to you.

On a number of occasions over the years I have said that something which always bothers me is the number of people who have tried to ridicule me when I have frankly explained some of my methods. Letters have appeared in the angling press to the effect that Ivan Marks must think some of us have just fallen off a Christmas tree! Attitudes which are dismissive and sceptical can be very hurtful to a person who has tried to be honest and helpful towards others. Surely it stands to reason that I don't fish in every way just like everyone else; otherwise I should be the same as them, and have nothing new to contribute.

Already in this book we have been through the basics of float fishing and have looked in detail at individual floats and how I fish them. Now we are going to discuss the icing on the cake, the little details that so many people scoff at, but which I know for sure add up to more than everything else. They make me, if nothing else, an individual.

It might be a good idea to deal first with one of the most controversial issues – the advantages and disadvantages of using small hooks.

Small hooks

By now you will have appreciated the supreme importance of bait presentation in float fishing. And it's not difficult to realise the effect that the size and weight of a hook can have upon the way the bait is presented. To take a simple example, and a common one, ask yourself how a hook can affect the movement of a caster. However small the hook it will add weight to the caster, and therefore it will cause it to sink at a faster rate than casters which are thrown in as loose feed. The bigger the hook inside the caster, the more unnaturally it will cause it to behave in relation to the free offerings.

The difference does not end there. When a fish takes a caster it sucks it in and mouths it. If the fish is not particularly keen to feed it will reject any caster which behaves unnaturally while being taken. Those dithering, jabbing bites often experienced in caster fishing are sometimes caused by the weight of the hook, or its hard bulk inside the caster, putting the fish off at the last moment. At least, I believe this to be so, though in some cases the problem arises through a poor choice of float, or bad shotting.

There are plenty of people who will tell you how they've caught a stone or more of quality roach by putting the largest possible hook inside their casters, say a size 14. And of course this can happen. What you don't hear about is the number of times they've failed to catch at all using this method. When

the fish are really feeding you can get away with murder; but
on hard-fished match waters it's invariably a constant battle
to get them interested.

Small hooks also cause the minimum of damage to maggots, allowing them to behave naturally in the water or on
the river bed. And it is worth bearing in mind that on many
waters the fish have learned to be suspicious of any bait
attached to a hook. The smaller the hook the less they are
suspicious; your ratio of bites increases and the bites you get
are more confident and easier to hit.

Small, of course, is a relative term; it depends on what you
regard as big. Some anglers feel that a size 14 hook is small.
Me, I'd describe a 22 as being small, a 20 as being normal, an
18 as big, a 16 as enormous and . . . well, I can't really think of
a word to describe a 14! I'm not sure I've seen one for years.

Granted that small hooks produce more bites, then some
people would say that they lose too many fish. I have never
found this to be true. Certainly a big bream on a 20 can't be
bullied into the landing net, simply because the hook-hold
cannot be very deep. But a well-set size 20 takes a very firm
grip and with care you can land quite big fish without worry.

I ought to mention, of course, that I'm not recommending
small hooks for big baits such as bread flake or luncheon
meat. I'm referring to baits such as maggots and casters on
which I rely so much. Even then, if I put on a red worm when
bream fishing, I'm quite happy to use a size 18 or 20 hook.
I'm just a small-hook addict, hooked on them if you like! You
can take it for granted that I automatically associate all the
float-fishing techniques in this book with the use of small
hooks – my sort of small!

Good bait

This can't be emphasised too much. Even if your float, hook, shotting and bait presentation are all perfect, you won't get good bites unless your bait is right. To realise why this is so depends on your understanding how fish feed in waters which are heavily fished.

Point one is that the fish are seldom hungry. Many anglers are guilty of over-feeding and what with all the groundbait, loose-feed and natural food in waters the fish are hardly ever ravenous. Now consider yourself. When you are really hungry you could just about eat anything. You wouldn't pause to inspect your food, you'd just wolf it down. But let's say you'd been eating pretty well and didn't particularly want any more food. Then you'd be much more difficult to please, and you would want the food to be both tempting and small.

Or look at it another way. You're in a room, surrounded by food, and you're not really hungry. What you would probably do is wander round rather choosily and finally select the most tempting morsel you could see. Fish are just the same; I almost said they're only human! Treat them as having a bit of sense and you'll catch a lot more of them.

Point two is that on still and slow-moving waters the fish have plenty of time to inspect your bait. They can nudge it, mouth it and generally sample it before actually deciding whether to take it. Those half-hearted knocks on your float that never develop into a hittable bite are very often caused by indifferent fish playing with a third-rate bait. In the end they leave it.

Yes, I have heard about the days when the fish go mad, when they're queuing up for your bait and you can catch them on anything from tomato skins to old socks. I haven't experienced many days like that myself, and I certainly don't fish in anticipation of such once-in-a-lifetime events.

The third point concerns bringing your bait to the attention of the fish. If you are feeding the same bait as your hook-bait, you must feed carefully. Otherwise the chance of

your hook-bait being picked up in preference to all the free
offerings is reduced in proportion to the amount of feed you
throw in. Also, you are in danger of over-feeding the fish so
that they lose interest altogether. This applies particularly
when you are fishing casters for roach. Bream, of course, can
hoover up vast quantities of bait and are not so easily put off.
One way in which you can make the fish notice your bait is to
make it different from your feed. For example, you can feed
with squatts and use gozzers for hook-bait. Or you can feed
casters and use a red worm, or a worm and caster cocktail,
for hook-bait. It will then stand out as a special offering
among your loose-feed.

My normal baits are maggots of various kinds, casters and
red worms, and I insist that they are fresh, clean and in
first-class condition. If they are old, or stale or sour, they are
worse than useless and I would not use them, They need to
be soft and succulent so that fish don't reject them before
registering bites. In match fishing particularly, the quality of
bait can be a key factor. After all, if food was free, you'd
quickly leave a cheap and nasty café if there was a good
restaurant next door. And that's what happens to the fish in
your swim if your bait is poor and the man at the next peg
can offer a much better menu.

Not only are fish far from hungry, they also develop a
certain amount of suspicion about baits. On hard-fished
waters they may well have been caught several times before,
and therefore if there is anything wrong with your bait
presentation, or with the feel and taste of your bait, the fish
will not take it.

The belief that feed attracts fish to your swim is not one I
share to any great extent; for me the use of feed is to hold fish
that are in your swim and encourage them to start feeding.
The first part of this process, holding the fish in front of you
for as long as possible, can only be achieved by using top-

quality bait. The second part, encouraging the fish to feed, depends very much on how and when you introduce that feed.

Feeding the swim

I have already dealt with this important technique in Chapter 7 of my book on match fishing, and I don't propose to repeat all that information here. What I must do, however, is point out how feeding the swim is a vital part of every aspect of float fishing.

If you have been following everything carefully so far, you should now be in a position to fish a given situation with a sensibly chosen float, correct shotting, a small hook and top-quality hook-bait. When the fish are feeding, that combination should give you bold, deliberate bites that are an answer to every angler's prayer. But don't forget the first part of the sentence – *when the fish are feeding*. Because when they're not, the best tackle and technique in the world are not going to catch them.

This is where the art of feeding the swim comes in. Sometimes there are days when you can't make it work, when you just can't catch. It could be there are no fish in your swim, though more likely it's caused by some natural factor that you can't understand. Even the best anglers haven't got all the answers, thank goodness.

But there are many days when an expert angler will catch fish and the novice won't through no other reason than that the expert has the skill to build up his swim by intelligent feeding. To do this well requires experience, maybe even instinct. I must admit that there are times when I decide to change my feeding pattern on what seems at the time like a hunch. And it pays off. But it happens too often for it to be luck, so probably it's based on experience. John Goodwin always says that I think like a fish, and that's how I know. And maybe he's right. Who knows?

The main point is that you should not get too despondent if you seem to be float fishing correctly and are not getting bites. Either nothing will induce the fish to feed, in which case it's not your fault, or you are making some mistake in your feeding, and with practice that can be put right. It is most important for you to understand that the perfecting of one technique, e.g. a float-fishing style, does not always mean that that technique *in isolation* will enable you to catch. All too often one technique depends for its success on the perfecting of another that goes hand in hand with it. Float fishing and feeding are classic examples of two interdependent techniques.

Mistakes in feeding are most commonly related either to the amount of feed or to the timing of the feeding, or to both in bad cases. There are four basic errors:

a) Feeding too heavily
b) Feeding too lightly, or not at all   } Amount

c) Feeding when you shouldn't
d) Not feeding when you should   } Timing

Once you've got the basics right you can proceed to more sophisticated considerations, such as the best kind of feed to use in particular circumstances, or whether to use ground-bait or loose feed.

If it were easy to know how to feed correctly, everybody would be able to do it. Certainly some general advice can be given, such as feeding to the number of fish you believe to be in your swim, or, in most float-fishing situations, feeding little and often, a constant pattern. But only experience will tell you how to get it right nine times out of ten. Getting it right ten times out of ten involves having some mystic communion with the fish themselves. Perhaps I can sum up the problems like this: if you could say that the biggest crime is *over*-feeding, then the second biggest crime is *under*-feeding. Think about it!

Making the right decisions

It is impossible to begin float fishing without first having made a number of decisions. Unless you possess only one float you must have made a choice, for some reason; you will also have decided on the depth you want to fish, and the initial distribution of your shotting. Not only that, but most likely you are setting out to catch a particular species of fish, and you will be casting a certain distance out. Unless you are in a match you will also have decided where you want to fish, and even at what time of the day.

For an angler, good decisions mean he catches, bad decisions mean he doesn't. The pleasure angler has more freedom to make the best decisions and he is less likely to suffer from his mistakes. The match angler, by contrast, has less freedom and will usually be made to pay for his mistakes, in every sense! Therefore, as a match angler, I am very aware of the importance of making the right decisions, because to be consistently successful in match fishing means that you must not only decide correctly, but also as early as possible; preferably more quickly than anyone else.

Decisions are based on knowledge, and knowledge comes mostly through experience. This is why practising is important, it is why the more you fish the more you learn, if you have any intelligence at all. If a man bought a stick float and didn't know what it was designed for, he might just do something stupid like trying to fish it bottom only with a strong downstream wind in twelve feet of turbulent water. It would be a disastrous decision, but unless he was a fool would never make the same mistake again.

Experience, learning the hard way if you like, is invaluable; but there are other ways of learning. You can get help from other people, you can watch other people, you can read books and you can generally go out of your way to get hold of information.

Although I have a great deal of experience I never underestimate the value of listening to other people. I don't mean I believe everything they say, but I will always listen. One lifetime is too short to find out everything there is to know even about fishing. I've often said that I can learn something from even the youngest lad, and it's true.

One of my policies is to find out as much as I can by myself, by actually fishing. But I spend a lot of time walking and talking to other anglers. If I have to fish a match on a stretch of water that I don't know enough about I will try to get some reliable information from friends and contacts. When I sit down to fish a match I like to feel I have done my homework in every possible way.

It is only by building up knowledge and experience that you can hope to arrive at the right decisions first time. As far as float fishing goes I even have to decide whether to float fish at all – maybe legering would be a more productive method. And if I do opt for float fishing my decision over which style to choose will be influenced by my knowledge of the water, the particular stretch I am fishing, the kind of fish I expect to catch and whereabouts I expect to catch them. I may then find that conditions on the day, such as the position and strength of the wind, or the speed of the flow, will force me to adapt to some extent the technique I would have used in ideal conditions.

OK, I've started fishing. But I was wrong, I'm not catching. Then I have to try and work out why I was wrong and what I need to do to put things right. Maybe I need to fish more heavily, or further out. Perhaps the depth or shotting is wrong. Experience will help me to find the answer in the shortest possible time – if there is an answer.

One of the great things about fishing is that, all things being equal, you get better with time. Gradually you find by a kind of instinct that you are making the right decisions more often, and more quickly. Only if you are static will you fail to improve. But you can accelerate your rate of improvement if you have an inquiring mind and think about what you are doing.

There's just one thing in fishing that is rather special to the sport and stops a lot of people making progress. It's this: in so many other sports the novice has no option but to admit that his lack of success is due to lack of skill. He knows he can't drive a golf ball 200 yards, he knows he can't win a world boxing championship, he knows he couldn't dribble a football past five defenders and score a spectacular goal from the edge of the penalty area. He admits these things because he has to. In fishing, it can be different. He can produce all sorts of excuses to hide his lack of ability: the weather was wrong, it was too hot, it was too cold, there were no fish where he was, and so on. Therefore, in fishing most especially, the important thing is to be honest with yourself, be humble, be prepared to admit it to yourself if you've made a mistake. Only then will you be in a position to turn your bad decisions into advantages – by learning from them.

Confidence

Any successful angler will tell you that confidence is half the battle. And of course success brings confidence and lack of success destroys it. It's a kind of vicious circle where lack of confidence causes you to fish badly and in turn have even less confidence. In match fishing a run of bad draws can shake the confidence of even the best anglers, and once lost it takes some finding again.

I've often said that confidence is the invisible man at my side who is more help to me than everything else added together. It's amazing how something which is no more than an attitude of mind can make such a difference to my fishing. It may sound silly, but if I start fishing in a certain way and just *know*, inside me, that I'm going to catch, then nine times out of ten I do. Unfortunately, the opposite is true. Why should this be?

Well, there's one thing certain, the fish don't know how you're feeling. What's going on inside your mind isn't going to affect their inclination to feed one little bit. But the effect of your attitude on how you fish can be considerable, even though you don't realise it at the time. Fishing with casters on some waters, like the Welland, is a good example of where confidence is essential. Sometimes it's a case of sacrificing the first hour or two of a match in order to take a big weight later on. This requires confidence in your method, your skill and your decisions. The angler who lacks confidence chops and changes nervously from one line to another, from float fishing to legering, even from one bait to the other. He's constantly re-casting instead of waiting for his bait to achieve the correct presentation. All in all he doesn't really believe he's going to catch later on, and as a result he doesn't.

Perhaps you're thinking that it's all very well for me to think this way because I've proved I can do it. The trouble is that until you *believe* you can do it, you most likely never will. Maybe I look sometimes as though I'm so easy-going that I'm not bothered whether I catch or not; but it isn't true. Underneath I still have self-belief – must have. Without it I am finished.

The same is true for you. Learn the basics, practise the techniques, do your homework. Without these things you will always have a bingo mentality towards your fishing. Gradually your confidence will grow and you must do everything you can not to let any failures destroy it. Of all the things in fishing this is the hardest to explain, and some people laugh at the whole idea. But for me it's nearly everything and when my confidence is high I just about believe I could empty the river. And that is when I perform.

Bait presentation

I'd like to bring together at this stage a number of aspects of float fishing that I've already discussed:

a) choice and control of float;
b) amount and distribution of shotting;
c) depth;
d) size of hook.

Now these are all considerations that I take very seriously, yet they are also the very details that some people say are overrated. But there is one crucial thing that these four factors have in common, along with the diameter of the line, and it is this: together they determine absolutely the *way in which your bait is presented to the fish*. And nothing, but nothing, is more important than this.

Let me put it like this. If you begin fishing by using a certain float in a certain way, at a certain depth, with a pattern of shotting, a certain sized hook and a particular breaking strain line, then any single tiny alteration in any of these details, even moving a small shot a matter of inches, would in some way alter your bait presentation. And this in turn will frequently alter your bite rate, either for better or worse. This fact is not a secret, but it might just as well be one for all the people who are not prepared to accept it. I am, of course, speaking as a match angler whose main concern is to get bites, and I don't just think, I *know*, that bait presentation must be the final, perfect end in a long chain of details and techniques.

What this all means is that to master the art of float fishing you must pay great attention to all the details. If you just can't believe that the details matter, then you can't make progress. It's very much an attitude of mind. Two anglers can be fishing a big river and catching nothing. The first one thinks, 'There aren't any fish here.' The second one thinks, 'There's bound to be some fish here. It's just that they won't take my bait in the way I'm presenting it to them.' He will experiment and most likely he will begin to catch. Perhaps after an hour he won't get any more bites. But he won't think, 'All my fish have gone away.' He'll think, 'My fish are feeding in a different way now.' And he'll work out the answer – different bait presentation. The first angler will sit biteless through all this and then go home and tell his wife how a lucky angler next to him was drawn on a pile of fish. Of course, there will be some days when even the second angler will fail, either because the fish can't be induced to feed, or because he never finds the answer. But because he realises the importance of bait presentation, and is constantly trying to improve it on the day, he will always be a better bet than the other man who waits all day for the fish to do things his way.

Thinking like a fish

I reckon if I really was a fish, I'd take a bit of catching! I just happen to have this silly, unscientific idea that fish are a lot cleverer than people think. I give them credit for some cunning and intelligence, and I believe the way to learn to catch them is to be as smart as they are by trying to get inside their minds, find out how they work and then see if I can outwit them.

I really enjoy thinking like a fish, imagining how I'd react in different circumstances. It's one of my little hobbies. Yet a great deal of my approach to fishing is based upon it. I'll give you a few examples of what I mean. I say to myself:

> If I was a fish, I don't think I'd like to be pelted with great big balls of groundbait. I think I'd move on somewhere else.
> If I was a fish I'd be frightened by a lot of stamping and banging on the bank. I'd swim further out for some peace and quiet.
> If I was a fish and I ate a rotten caster, I wouldn't eat any more.
> If I was a fish I wouldn't be too keen to chew a bait and a dirty great hook at the same time.
> If I was a fish and I wasn't hungry, I wouldn't chase after food. It would have to be put nearly into my mouth, and even then I might not bother if it wasn't really tasty.

Sometimes I do it the other way round, and compare what goes on underwater with what goes on among people. Something like this: if I was eating out in a crowded restaurant and suddenly someone was dragged from a table kicking and screaming and thrashing about, I'd think twice about staying to finish my food. If it happened again to someone else, we'd all probably leave in a hurry. On the other hand, if that person had been quickly and quietly removed, we'd hardly notice. Therefore, if I hook a fish in a shoal I try to get it out of the shoal immediately and then play it some distance away where it won't upset the others.

You see, I have this idea that fish are sensible sort of creatures, rather like us, and they react to basic situations in a natural, instinctive way. Their instinct to survive is perhaps the strongest, and therefore suspicion and fear are their normal reactions to what is unusual or unnatural.

If I was a fish I'd think twice before swimming across a carpet of white groundbait.

Of course some fish, like some people, are stupid, and they're easy to catch. But with a little thought, preferably fishy, you can catch the smart ones as well!

There must once have been a cartoonist who had the same idea as I have because he drew a cartoon in which a father fish was ticking off a baby fish for trying to eat a maggot suspended in the water with a great hook in it. The father fish took the baby fish aside and pointed to the maggot. 'Now, son,' he said, 'when you see one of these hanging like that, never eat it. But don't go far away, because sooner or later some fool will throw in a handful of them for nothing.'

If I was a fish, I'd agree with that! I'd expect better bait presentation.

Doing it daft!

If mastering float fishing takes three stages, then doing it daft has got to be the last one, the final straw so to speak. A lot of people never make stage three because they're too sensible!

Stage one is learning the simple basics; stage two is putting them into practice, refining them until you have perfect technique; stage three is forgetting all you learned in the first two stages. Let me explain further before we all go mad.

Right, you've learned the basics of trotting a stick float in the classic style. You know the fish will be facing upstream, that it's your job to control your tackle delicately so that the float, fished over-depth, is held slightly back to enable the bait to rise gently just off bottom and travel down the swim. You know that when you do this the bait will be ahead of the float and shots and you will more or less steer it into the waiting mouths of the roach hovering in the stream. Just like the book says!

You practise this until you're so good at it you're thinking in terms of international selection. People watching you think you've got that float on a piece of invisible elastic. You've arrived!

But you've only arrived half-way. Why? Because there are not only some days when this technique won't produce bites, there are days when *your very perfection at it stops you getting bites you would otherwise have had!* So, you've got to learn to be able to do it daft as well. If traditional trotting methods fail you may well find me letting the float go, 'running it at 'em' as we say, even encouraging drag and generally causing all kinds of atrocities to affect the bait presentation.

You might well ask why a fish which has turned its nose up at a well-presented bait should suddenly decide to feed when the bait is presented in an unnatural manner. And I can't tell you the answer. All I know is that it can happen, and that knowledge can be vital on certain days. Let me give you an example.

A few years ago I was fishing a match on the Welland and conditions were ideal for using a Zoomer – steady flow, slight upstream wind. Now, as you know, I fish my Zoomer top and bottom, which means that the line remains on the surface of the water. This is why the Zoomer, fished my way, can only work properly in favourable wind conditions.

On this particular day, although things were working perfectly, I wasn't catching. Then the wind suddenly got stronger and began to blow my float upstream *against* the current. On a slow-moving water like the Welland this would give a ridiculously unnatural bait presentation, and I was about to change tackle when I had a bite. After that the match was a formality and I finished well clear with a good weight of bream, all caught by doing it daft. I had broken all the rules of Zoomer fishing and it paid off.

In my book on match fishing I mentioned this incident,

and how some other anglers had tried to fish correctly by
using antenna floats and sunken lines. They didn't catch
because the fish didn't want it that way on that particular
day. But there is an interesting sequel to the story.

Later that year I did the same thing again, and I thought I
was onto something. But the following year I tried the same
tactic on several occasions and it didn't produce. Even so, I
didn't forget, and in 1976 I won another Welland match the
same way. I have now decided that on some Fenland waters
in *certain years* for some reason this is a deadly method. 1976
was such a year, and every time conditions were right – or
wrong, if you like! – I made that technique pay.

So, over the years, I have proved that fishing a Zoomer
correctly can be a killing method for bream – and I have also
proved that fishing a Zoomer *incorrectly* can be just as effective *at the right time*. Now, I haven't a clue why this should be
so – all I need to know is that it is. And whereas some anglers
stop when they have learned how to fish a method correctly,
the top anglers have an edge because they are prepared to
break the rules.

I get a particular pleasure from winning a match by doing
it daft, especially when anglers around me are fishing
according to the book. Not this one, of course! Mind you, it
doesn't happen all that often, and most times a traditional
technique will produce more fish. That's why we all need the
basics. The point is that you must always remember that the
fish haven't been taught and just occasionally they will
forget the rules. That's when you should be doing it daft, like
fishing four feet deep in twelve feet of water, or changing
your float for one of my matchsticks.

Really, of course, doing it daft is only a proper description
of breaking *your own* rules. The fish don't find it daft at all
because on those special days it gives them the kind of bait
presentation they want. I never have been much of a one for

laying down rules at the best of times, and this is probably why I enjoy getting results sometimes by doing things differently. What was it somebody once said? 'Rules are for the strict obedience of fools and the guidance of wise men.' If this is true where float fishing is concerned, I'd like to be thought of as belonging to the wise men.

Versatility

If you follow all the advice I have offered so far, you should automatically be aware of how important it is to be versatile in your float fishing. This doesn't just apply to technique; it also applies to different kinds of waters.

There are some anglers who practise so hard on their local waters that they become really expert at fishing them. I won't say they're unbeatable, but their local knowledge is such that they're always a threat in any match. However, if you take some of them to a different water in another part of the country they would be lost.

For someone fishing for pleasure locally, it doesn't matter that their experience is limited. But a match angler cannot afford to be out of his depth as soon as he's asked to fish outside his own patch. One week I may be fishing a fast river like the Trent or the Severn; the next week a wide Fenland water such as the Welland or the Nene; and the week after that could see me on a stillwater. So, the ability to be able to change with equal confidence from a stick float to a 3½ swan shot antenna, or anything in between, is vital.

I would never say that I am the best angler at fishing a particular float style on a particular water. But I do say that I'm pretty useful at fishing any style on any water, which is a different thing. It's really the art of all-round float fishing. It's versatility.

Practice

I don't enjoy pleasure fishing, so when I'm not fishing a
match I'll be practising for a future match. And this isn't
really pleasure fishing because I'm not always trying to
catch as many fish as I can.

Practising for me is learning not only what methods will
work, but finding out how others compare. If I'm catching
fish at a reasonable rate I will deliberately alter my tackle to
see what effect this has on my catching rate. Very often this
involves moving shot and depth. Or maybe I'll deliberately
choose to fish a line which I would not normally regard as the
best one, just to see what happens. If one or two friends are
with me, and they usually are, we can compare the effective-
ness of one method with the other.

Generally my policy is to establish the most successful
techniques for a given water at various times during the
season. That is step one. Step two is then to see what other
methods are productive if the favourite one should fail. Step
three involves trying to discover a further approach which
will be better than any of the others. And for the match
angler who wants to keep at the top, step three is a must.

For one thing, waters change from season to season, and
the whole process has to be re-established each year. The
permutations in float fishing involve baits, feeding patterns,
line, depth and shotting, and although any necessary
seasonal alterations to these things are often small, there can
be times when the change needs to be radical. For example,
three years ago some dredging operations along the far bank
of the Welland caused major changes in the location of some
fish, especially the bream shoals.

There is a strong temptation when practising to carry on
catching once a successful method has been found. But that
is only step one. And it is when you are catching and know

the fish are there that you can best proceed to steps two and three. So resist the temptation simply to sit catching all day on the one method.

A further temptation is to choose to fish a swim where you expect to catch a lot of fish. This should be avoided, too, unless your confidence needs a boost. It's those other swims you need to work at, the ones where you have to work hard to catch your fish.

Details

Details are little things which on their own don't seem very important. For example, a speck of dust doesn't look as though it could have any significance, but if it happened to be blocking a tiny jet in the carburettor of your car you might think differently. Ten thousandths of an inch seems a detail too, but if the gaps on your sparking plugs were each increased by that amount it would make an enormous difference to your engine.

Because I appreciate the importance of detail I spend a lot of my time doing silly little things. Or, at least, that's what some people call them. I've been ridiculed in the past for drawing people's attention to details – for example, when I pointed out that if maggots are hooked correctly, you can expect more bites. By correctly I meant so that the maggot can crawl naturally on its correct surface. The whole idea seemed to make some people fall about laughing, saying I was having them on.

If you take a small point in isolation, it's possible to make fun of it. But when details are seen in context, together, they add up to a lot more than the sum of their parts. I look at it this way: the general truths of fishing are known by quite a lot of anglers but it's the little points that can make all the difference. For example, if you hook a worm in the middle, so that it hangs in equal parts from the hook, on a day when the bream are only sucking at the bait you may never catch at all. But if you hook it at one end, you should at least hit one bite in two. Why? Because the fish sucks in part of the worm and toys with it, and if your hook is at one end of the worm there is a fifty-fifty chance that it will be in the fish's mouth during that time. But if the hook is in the middle of the worm it may never be taken at all if the fish is just sucking and nibbling at one end. Just a little thing – but important.

I can get a lot of pleasure from details – they fascinate me. Nothing is so small that I would consider it unimportant. When I catch fish I couldn't catch before, simply by moving a number 6 shot a couple of inches, or by adding a micro-dust shot to the hook length, or by changing from a size 20 to a size 22 hook, I am a happy man. It encourages me to keep playing about with other silly little things that on a certain day may help me to catch fish when other people are struggling.

There's just one more thing, and then I do believe I've told you the lot. And it's this. I just about eat, drink and sleep fishing. You could call me a professional because it's my whole life and 90 per cent of my work as well. And I can't really expect everyone else to be in that position. I'm a lucky man.

But what you can do is put as much into your fishing as you can. Try to keep up with what's happening – read the press, read books, talk to other anglers. And, dare I mention it, actually go fishing as often as possible. In this respect it helps no end if you can find a wife who will put up with it. I happen to have one, and I can thoroughly recommend them!

Postscript
by John Goodwin

'LIKE WINE, almost, he seems to get better every year.' It is
almost three years ago that I made this comment about
Ivan's continuing successes right through the sixties and
early seventies. I wrote it in July 1974.

It is now March 1977, and the remark remains as true as
ever. In the last six months Ivan has been runner-up in the
World Championship and was voted Angler of the Year by
the readers of the national weekly *Angling Times*. Why is this
so? Big names come, and big names go, in angling rather as
in the worlds of pop music or football. But for at least ten
years now Ivan Marks has been at the very top of his
profession.

In this book he has tried to explain his knowledge and
methods of float fishing, the thing he does best of all. And I,
at least, have found it fascinating to see how an angler of his
exceptional talent works out and overcomes all the problems
which he, along with the rest of us, is constantly coming up
against when float fishing. His thinking should knock on the
head for all time any suggestion that he is a lucky-dip angler
with the golden hand at the draw-bag. He is one the most
thinking, and original, anglers alive today.

Most of the qualities that have made him a great angler for

so many years have emerged through his two books – natural
skill, brilliant technique, deep knowledge, originality, to
mention but a few. But there is one quality which is perhaps
the most important of all when explaining *how he continues to be
so good year after year*. Because I take that to be the judgment of
time between those who are just good and those who are
great. 'Time', they say, 'will tell.' And in Ivan's case it has
told, most emphatically, that he is no flash in the pan. He is
the genuine article.

Now, this particular quality Ivan has is not one that I
think he himself is aware of. But those who know him well
will know what I mean when I say that *he has this remarkable
ability to insulate himself from any consideration not to do with fishing*.
He admits himself that fishing is his life, but I don't think he
realises how wonderfully he manages to ignore just about
everything else. It's as if subconsciously he realises that his
total involvement in fishing is *the* essential factor to his
continuing success, and somehow he has succeeded in wrap-
ping up this essential involvement and not letting the worries
and problems of everyday life get at it and harm it.

In this way I regard him as an eccentric. Try and tackle
him about something not connected with fishing and he
switches off. Not interested. 'I don't know', he'll say, 'you'll
have to ask Roy.' What he really means is that he doesn't
want to know. But if I ring him up and ask him how the
Nene's fishing, he'll come alive at once and run me up a
phone bill that I daren't think about.

It works something like this. Last time Ivan came to stay
with me, Roy Marlow made all the arrangements, as usual.
Then Linda, Ivan's wife, drove the car the eighty-odd miles
to my house. Ivan was asleep. As soon as he arrived he was
anxious to start fishing. He never stopped fishing or talking
about fishing from then on. At one point Linda remarked
that she was making more garden space, and I foolishly

asked if Ivan would be doing the digging. 'I can't,' he said. 'I might damage my hands!'

And so it goes on. Ivan goes his own way, lives in his own little world, and shuts out everything else. This is why he has been at the top so long, and it is also why he has remained amiable and unsoured through the years. Always cheerful, always helpful, always modest – his popularity only equalled by his achievements. He is a great character as well as a great angler who fishes forever as the rest of the world passes by.

Index

'Angler of the Year', 169
Angling Times, 23, 102, 169
Antenna floats, 21, 23, 24, 28, 41, 92-147
  2 mm (short, canal), 108-110
  2 mm loaded canal, 108, 110-112
  2 mm (long, canal), 108, 112-114
  Slimlines, 108, 114-116
Antenna, tipped, 13, 17, 28, 45, 75
Arrow floats, 60, 80-83, 84
Avon float, 28, 53, 67-71

Back-shotting, 40
Bait presentation, 29, 38, 74, 95, 125, 146, 159-160, 164
Bait, quality of, 150-153
Balance of floats, 47, 49
Balsa floats, 27, 28, 52, 53, 71-75, 82
Basics of float fishing, 26-49
Bassi, Dino, 24, 25

Bites, 30-32, 33
  on the drop, 30, 58-59, 110, 112, 113, 116, 119
  lift, 30-31, 86, 110, 116, 146
  registration, 94-95
Blackwater, River, 64
Bloodworm, 100

Caps, float, 46
Carrot float, 60-63
Casters, 13, 14, 16, 17, 32, 59, 100, 149, 152, 158
Casting, 33-34, 44-45, 56, 129, 137, 144
CIPS, 96
Collins, Peter, 26
Confidence, 157-159
Continental style, 24, 38, 96-101
Crowquill float, 21, 27

Dart floats, 60, 105-108, 116, 122
Decisions, making the right, 155-157

Depth, importance of, 30, 31,
    37-39, 98-99
Details, importance of, 167
'Doing it daft', 162-165
Ducker floats, 53, 84-88, 90, 91,
    131

Experimenting, importance of,
    35-37

Favourite floats, 29, 47
Feeding, 34-35, 37, 43, 46,
    153-154
Fenland waters, 88, 92, 122,
    164, 165
Float fishing, brief history of
    development of, 20, 21
Float fishing, long-range,
    42-47, 121-123, 126

Goodwin, John, 102, 153
Gozzers, 152
Great Ouse Relief Channel,
    129, 136

Harris, Robin, 86
Hemp, 16, 100
Hooks, small, 149-150
Huntspill, 136

Javelin float, 108, 116-119, 121

Ladbroke's Super League, 25
Lane, Billy, 21, 84, 136
Line, choosing a, 34-35
Lock-shot, 45, 110, 123, 126
Luncheon meat, 71, 150

Marks, Christopher, 22

Marks, Linda, 22, 23, 170
Marksman float, 103-105, 107
Marlow, Roy, 22, 23, 170
Matchstick float, 19, 49,
    101-102, 107
'Mending' your line, 40
Missile float, 45, 133-137, 144
Mousedropping lead, 100-101

National Championships, 20,
    107, 136
Nene, 88, 92, 116, 136, 165

Pacemaker floats, 39, 52, 63-67,
    69, 80
Pasinetti, Fausto, 24
Pole fishing, 24, 25, 28, 96-101
Porcupine quill float, 27
Practice, 166

Reels, 40
Reverse ducker floats, 131-133
Rods, 32-33
Rolfe, Johnny, 78
Running-water floats, 53-91

Sarkanda reed antenna floats,
    126-129, 142
Severn, 25, 27, 64, 71, 165
Shot, classifications, 51
Shot, numbering, 50
Shot, working, 18, 51-52
Shotting, 29-30, 31, 41
    for pole float, 98-101
    for antenna floats, 123-126
Sliders, 136, 137
Special Balsa floats, 25, 96-101,
    102, 103, 107
Squatts, 152

Stick floats, 21, 28, 29, 39, 42, 53-59, 60, 63, 64, 67, 78, 103, 122, 155, 162

Still and slow-moving water floats, 92-147

Surface skim, 28, 46, 78, 92, 108

Swinger float, 41, 53, 75-80, 82, 84, 90

Swingtip, 21

Tangles, preventing, 33, 45, 123, 137

Tares, 16, 17

Thinking like a fish, 160-162

Tipped Sarkanda reed antenna floats, 129-131, 142

Tipped Swinger floats, 108, 119-121

Tipped Zoomer floats, 119, 139-142

Trent, 25, 39, 88, 91, 165

Trotting, 39-52
 reverse, 75, 85-88, 91

Under-tow, 93-94

Versatility, 165

Waggler float, 28, 39, 41, 53, 69, 84, 88-91, 105, 133

Warwickshire Avon, 25, 91

Wasp grub, 71

Weight (i.e. use of lead), 21, 48, 74

Welland, 25, 42, 91, 137, 144, 158, 163, 164, 165, 166

Witham, 15, 16, 25, 90, 91, 102, 136

World Championships, 20, 24, 25, 96, 101, 169

Wye, 64

Zoomer float, 21, 25, 42, 45, 49, 54, 122, 123, 133, 137-139, 163, 164
 Ivan's Special, 142-146